D1159624

New England Invite

FRESH FEASTS TO SAVOR THE SEASONS

KATE BOWLER

Globe
Pequot

Guilford, Connecticut

Globe
Pequot

An imprint of The Rowman & Littlefield Publishing Group, Inc.
4501 Forbes Blvd., Ste. 200
Lanham, MD 20706
www.rowman.com

Distributed by NATIONAL BOOK NETWORK

British Library Cataloguing in Publication Information available

Library of Congress Cataloging-in-Publication Data

Names: Bowler, Kate, 1985- author.
Title: New England invite : fresh feasts to savor the seasons / Kate Bowler.
Description: Guilford, Connecticut : Globe Pequot, 2018. | Includes index. |
  Identifiers: LCCN 2018011250 (print) | LCCN 2018012552 (ebook) | ISBN
  9781493034680 (e-book) | ISBN 9781493034673 (hardback : alk. paper)
Subjects: LCSH: Cooking, American—New England style. | Seasonal cooking. |
  LCGFT: Cookbooks.
Classification: LCC TX715.2.N48 (ebook) | LCC TX715.2.N48 B687 2018 (print) |
  DDC 641.5974—dc23
LC record available at https://lccn.loc.gov/2018011250

♾️™ The paper used in this publication meets the minimum requirements of American National Standard for Information Sciences—Permanence of Paper for Printed Library Materials, ANSI/NISO Z39.48-1992

Printed in the United States of America

TO MY MOM,

who taught me there's always room for one more

at the table, even if it means ordering pizza

CONTENTS

INTRODUCTION

THE BEST PLACE TO START IS ALWAYS AT THE BEGINNING. So I'd like to start by telling you how this book came to be. Once upon a time there was a young girl, just days out of college and sitting in her very first cubicle, browsing the depths of the Internet for creative inspiration. That young girl was me, and that was the beginning of my story. I started a blog and used it to chronicle my adventures in decorating, DIY projects, snippets of life with my family, and my never-ending experiments in the kitchen. It was a creative outlet, a casual hobby, a way to keep my brain and my hands busy on nights and weekends after I came home from a day job in marketing.

I've always been a documenter, a chronic journal keeper. My mom blames this tendency to need to record everything on my love of the book *Harriet the Spy* as a kid. I read it and told her afterwards that I needed to write down all of my observations in a notebook, just like Harriet. I suppose the blog was an extension of that obsession. I did just that; I wrote down my observations and thoughts and recipes. I wrote and wrote and wrote, and cooked and cooked and cooked, and over time my hobby turned into a food and lifestyle blog that I'm lucky enough to now call my career. I have the very fun task of thinking up recipes and sharing entertaining ideas and working with magazines to create the very type of content that I used to read in that small beige cubicle. It's been nearly a decade since I hit "publish" on that first blog post, and by some luck, that young girl who loved to cook and write found a way to make her dream job a reality.

As I was working to build Domestikatedlife.com over the past several years, there's always been a little something on the back burner that I was cooking up. (Yes, the pun was intended!) It was filling my notebooks, just like from my *Harriet the Spy* days, an idea for a book. I love to cook, and I love reading cookbooks. I love to entertain, and I love reading entertaining books. I have a huge collection of them; they fill a giant bookcase in my kitchen and they're tucked on shelves in every room of our house. I look at them for inspiration, for technique, for experimentation. Among all of those books though, I realized there wasn't one that really speaks to how I actually cook and entertain.

In my collection there are gourmet cookbooks that have complicated and intricately detailed recipes. They contain recipes that require skilled techniques and precision. I may attempt one of those recipes—with my breath held that it comes out okay—when I'm entertaining guests. But I'll lean on my old standby recipes to fill in the menu with things I am more comfortable with.

On the bookshelf there is also a collection of entertaining books that are aspirational and inspirational. They feature over-the-top tablescapes with colorful candy buffets, tall shiny candelabras, and layered sequined table linens. They are filled with images of Pinterest-quality parties that I would love to attend, but just don't go to in my real life. It makes me think I need to befriend more celebrities and attend more extravagant weddings so that I can indulge in these lavish celebrations.

I also love to thumb through cookbooks with that laid-back West Coast style, filled with images of beautiful chefs cooking in giant open kitchens with nothing but crisp, bright white walls in the background. I daydream about how lovely it must be to entertain on an airy, well-styled patio all year round because it never rains or snows. The pictures of the food look like modern art, with teeny-tiny portions and swirls of brightly colored purees. They are gorgeous, but those little plates look like I'd leave the party famished.

I own all of these books, and I love them and I read them often. They provide endless amounts of creative spark and inspiration for me. None of them, though, show how I really live and cook and entertain at our house, in our cute little coastal town in New England. At the heart of hosting, it's about making friends and family feel welcome and comfortable. It's casual and laid-back. We wear jeans, and guests dunk their hands in the cooler to grab their own drinks. Everything is served buffet-style—please help yourself and make yourself at home. Casual doesn't have to mean pizza and beer (though that is always a welcome menu at our house). I like to entertain in an unfussy way, but still with polish and thought and care.

This book is a collection of those real-life menus and how I truly host my friends and family at our home. It's inspired by my surroundings and the impact that the seasons have on how we live in New England. Everything is touched by the changing seasons here: what we wear, what we see, what we do with our free time, and especially what we eat and how we entertain. We bring pizza picnics to the beach on Friday nights all summer long. We relish in that first farmer's market of spring and fill up baskets of amazing ingredients that suddenly become available as the weather warms. We really know how to celebrate when the snow melts and the weather reaches patio-dining temperatures. We are tough and rugged and

endure chilly temperatures in the autumn to gather outside for pumpkin-carving parties on the porch and brisk strolls through the apple orchard. We will endure arctic temperatures for a good tailgating gathering. And we survive the winter by bringing the party inside, around the fireplace, and up into the mountains to make the most of those cozy snowy days. This book is organized by season for those many reasons. Each menu draws influence from how we live, and how we gather, as things change throughout the year. It's about making the most of each one, the food and the seasons, and it's exactly why I love living here.

When I started to write this book, I had two goals. One was to share delicious, simple recipes that I love to use in my real life. The other was to try to take a little bit of the intimidation out of entertaining. I'm here to dispel a few myths about cooking and hosting, and rebuff the excuses you may make for not entertaining. I promise, it's not as hard as it seems.

The first excuse you may make is "I do not have a picture-perfect kitchen." Let me assure you, you can do a lot with a little. I have a tiny kitchen with a decades-old electric stove that is terribly finicky, a very sensitive smoke detector nearby that goes off at least once a week when I'm cooking, and a small butcher block island that my husband made in the garage where I do most of my prep work. No restaurant-quality ranges or marble countertops were used in the making of this book; it was written and tested in a real-life home kitchen.

The same goes for fancy cooking tools and kitchen gadgets—for the most part you don't need much to make a good meal. I tried really hard to write these menus and recipes in a way that did not require any specialty tools. What you need is one good chef's knife, a saucepan, and some rimmed baking sheets. With those few items you can make nearly all the recipes in this book. Occasionally a mini food processor is involved or a pizza stone you may not already own. And yes, I do make a case at one point to go out and buy a $10 mini-donut pan, because then you can make mini donuts all the time at home, which is a very good reason to own one.

Another myth I'd like to bust is that you don't have the skills to cook a full menu for a party. You can do it, you can teach yourself just like I did. My only "professional" training comes from the school of grandma. Watching my Italian grandmother in the kitchen is the closest I've come to a cooking lesson. Like trying to learn any new skill, you just have to throw yourself into it and try. I read cookbooks, I watched online videos, I practiced and experimented to learn what I know about cooking. Even today when writing this cookbook, I'm still absorbing and learning and practicing. Get your hands dirty and give it a try, go ahead and make the recipes your own. Think a pasta dish needs more Parmesan cheese? Go for it, and drench it in cheese. It'll probably taste great, but you won't know until you try!

A lot of the intimidation around entertaining guests comes from not knowing where to start. That's why this book is organized by season, and within each seasonal section there are chapters for specific occasions. Every occasion in the book has a full menu to work from, with drinks, appetizers, entrees, desserts, and even some tips to bring it all together with approachable decor and table ideas. Pull inspiration from a full menu, or pick and choose the recipes that work for your tastes to make your own lineup.

The last myth to dispel is that you don't have the right occasion to host a party. There is a lot of pressure put on entertaining for a special event or holiday. You don't want to mess up Christmas. That can be traumatizing. People tell their therapists about ruined Christmases. So don't wait for a big occasion, start with entertaining at home today. Bring friends over for no other reason than just to get them together. Invite family over for a Sunday brunch or dinner to catch up. Make everyday occasions feel special with home cooking. This book is about drinking and eating well, but really it's about gatherings that bring together the people you love.

THE ENTERTAINING BASICS

PLAN THE MENU. You're entertaining guests and need to plan a menu for the party, but where do you start? For me, I like to consider two things first: the occasion and the season. The occasion usually helps answer a few key questions about what type of food you're going to serve. Is it a casual backyard gathering to celebrate someone's birthday? Is it a holiday party where guests will be coming and going throughout the afternoon? Is it a dinner party to welcome family from out of town? Once I have an idea of what the party will be, I can start narrowing down some menu choices. Next, I start to think about the season and what ingredients and dishes might work to highlight fresh ingredients. For a dinner menu, I might start with the protein in an entree and build around that central dish. For a casual afternoon gathering, I might pick a theme, like seafood, and brainstorm a series of recipes and bites that work together. The menu can also set the tone for the event, like offering small bites that encourage mixing and mingling in a casual setting. A heavier, plated entree signals a bit more of a formal celebration.

A good menu has balance. Toss around lots of ideas and then weigh how they might play off each other: warm appetizers versus cold appetizers, meat versus vegetarian options, light versus heavy ingredients. It's also a good idea to consider balance in how they'll be prepared, too. Try to pick a few dishes that can be prepared ahead of time, a few quick-assembly options, and only one or two recipes that require more time and focus the day of the event. The resulting food and drinks will come out much better if you can easily manage executing everything on the menu.

Perhaps the most important thing to consider when planning a menu is the guest list. Plan for allergies and likes and dislikes so that everyone feels welcome and well fed!

BUILD A PARTY-PREP TIMELINE. Have you ever been to a party where the hostess is frazzled in the kitchen? It's the worst. Sometimes things don't go as planned and a recipe fails or a dish gets forgotten and goes into the oven late. Then you start to scramble and the stress builds. It's happened to me, it's happened to everyone. One way I try to combat that harried state of frantic party preparations is to build a party-prep timeline.

My mother-in-law is an entertaining pro. She can execute a sit-down holiday dinner for forty-plus family members without even breaking a sweat. Everyone feels relaxed and welcome when attending a holiday celebration at their house, because she appears to do it with such ease. And while she makes it look so effortless, I know that it was actually a ton of hard work and organization and preparation that made it all happen. If you sneak into the kitchen while the holiday cooking is underway, you can see her detailed notes on the counter with a timeline for everything that needs to get done. It's a trick that I've borrowed from her and do every time I host a party now.

To build your party-prep timeline, scribble down every dish on your menu and make note of what can be prepped ahead of time. Write down how long each dish needs to be cooked and at what temperature. From there I start to organize all the information into a timeline. If the roast takes an hour to cook and fifteen minutes to rest and we plan to eat at

7 p.m., then the roast gets assigned a 5:45 p.m. time slot. If the green beans only need fifteen minutes to cook, but can be prepped in advance, I'll make a note in the morning to prepare the dish and another note at 6:45 p.m. to get them cooking. Can you make some of the appetizers in advance? Add them to the top of the timeline to work on the night before the party. It's like a run of show for a performance. The stove is the stage and each dish is a player in the well-choreographed routine.

I even like to add things to the timeline that aren't food related, like getting the ice onto the bar cart or giving the bathroom a final wipe down or lighting candles on the table. Building this road map for what needs to get done and exactly when it needs to happen takes a lot of the guess-work out of executing the meal. Following the timeline also means you'll be able to recover if and when something does go wrong! Remain calm and refer to your game plan.

PERFECT THE PARTY FLOW. My mom is the consummate hostess. She has great attention to detail and manages to put together just the right flowers, the right table linens, and the right menu, so that everything works together. More than anything, she knows how to make people welcome, which is why friends and family love coming to her parties. One of the biggest lessons I've learned from her is about how to create a party flow, or how to get guests moving and mixing and mingling. Where you build your bar or set up a dinner buffet or place appetizers has a big impact on how a gathering can flow.

Bar and food placement are typically the best ways to get your guests to where you want them to go. Put your bar setup far away from the front

door, which is usually where people congregate when they first arrive and cause a party traffic jam. Moving the bar farther into the space or into another room signals guests to flow in that direction since it's usually the first stop after they've entered a party. To keep the party moving and guests dispersed across the space, try setting up appetizers in a few different spots. At my mom's parties, snacks are spread out around different centralized conversation areas—the island, the dining table, the coffee table—and it keeps people moving and mingling and, most importantly, eating! If you're hosting a buffet around a dining room table or kitchen island, think about removing some of the chairs or bar stools that can hinder guests from gaining easy access to the meal.

Always think about the kids too. Our family friends host a big Christmas Eve party every year, and when we were little kids there were always trays of kid-friendly snacks for us in their playroom. There were pizza bagels and pigs in a blanket, and they were served on real plates and holiday trays that made us feel like we were part of the party, even if we were downstairs shooting each other with Nerf guns in the playroom.

THE TOOL KIT. I'm a bit of a collector when it comes to entertaining and serving pieces. It's part of the job; they come in handy for styling recipes! Despite a big collection of these items though, there are just a handful of items that I consistently rely on when hosting a party. I have a set of everyday white plates that I use, well, every day. No fancy wedding china, just plain old white dishes. They work for every occasion, every season, and every holiday. If I'm going to have a party with a theme or particular holiday color scheme, I'll bring in colored napkins to dress up the plain white plates. The same goes for the serving pieces I have in my pantry—big white bowls and platters that are workhorses and get pulled out every single time I entertain. The one specialty item that I think is worth having is a good, sturdy cake stand. It's a great way to add height to a buffet or make a simple appetizer look elevated. I won't tell you how many cake stands I own, because I've likely lost count. The other serving piece I use often isn't actually a serving piece at all, it's a big marble pastry board. I use it in the kitchen for baking and for rolling out pasta dough, but most often for creating a big cheese plate or appetizer platter.

Another versatile item I always keep in my entertaining tool kit is a set of mason jars. They can be used for so many things, like shaking up a quick salad dressing, holding some pretty fresh herb garnishes on the bar, or serving as individually portioned containers for desserts.

There are two types of glassware that I use when I'm hosting: glass tumblers and champagne flutes. The low glass tumblers are actually Spanish wine glasses, and I found them online after seeing them used at several restaurants. There's a good reason that you see them often in restaurants: They're incredibly versatile. They work for serving red wine or white wine, you can use them as water glasses, and you can even serve mixed drinks in them too. Champagne flutes are the other type of glassware that I always have on hand, because there is nothing more festive than a glass of cold, bubbly prosecco served in a real glass champagne flute. Mimosas in the morning, champagne at lunch, or a sparkling cocktail before dinner, you can pull them out for any event to make an occasion feel a little more special.

Keeping your pantry party-ready makes entertaining on the fly easier. Sometimes friends pop by on a Sunday afternoon to say hello, and I like to always be prepared with some drinks and bites to make people feel welcome. Nuts and crackers are easy things to keep in your cabinets, and I nearly always have a block of cheddar cheese in our fridge for a quick cheese plate. We live close to the ocean, so in the summer we get our fair share of weekend guests that come to see us and enjoy the nearby beach access. I keep sour cream in the fridge to make an easy summer dip with herbs and garlic. Serve it with some fresh veggies, which can easily be repurposed in a weeknight dinner if you don't use them all up. In the winter months, puff pastry in the freezer is a secret weapon for whipping up quick appetizers when family swings by for a holiday visit.

In nearly every recipe in this book, with the exception of some of the sweets, I use three ingredients that are a must to have on hand: olive oil, sea salt, and black pepper. They're used so often in my kitchen that I have all three in grabbing distance of my stove and workspace at all times.

My favorite cooking tools are simple. I have one good chef's knife that I rely on daily. A few wooden spoons and spatulas for mixing and scraping and stirring are always essential, and a quality pair of tongs is the item I grab most often from my crock of utensils. I always keep a box of individually cut pieces of parchment paper on hand for easy cleanup when baking appetizers and desserts, as it's a lifesaver for making quick work of getting things in and out of the oven. You don't need much to make it work; just stick with the basics.

PRE-PARTY CHECKLIST. You've got a guest list, a menu, and a timeline; it's almost time to party! Every time I entertain guests, I run through a little pre-party checklist to ensure I'm organized and my house is ready. It helps me feel ready to welcome friends and family, and actually enjoy the party myself!

The night before the party I do a quick clutter sweep, putting toys away and organizing things that are scattered around the house. I vacuum all the rooms (except for the kitchen, I get messy while I cook!), write my party-prep timeline for the next day, and take out and clean all the glassware. (This is my least favorite task.)

The morning of the party I take a look at my menu and pull out the serving dishes that I need for each item on the list. I set them out on the table or counter where I'm going to be serving food to get a layout of how I want things to be organized (think about party flow!), and then place a sticky note on each serving piece with the food item that it will hold. Next I tidy up the bathrooms and give the counters and mirror a wipe down (just kidding, I never do this—my husband always does because he's the best). If the party is in a cooler month, I take a minute to clear off the coat rack or put a few empty hangers in the coat closet for guests' jackets.

During the afternoon of the party I work on all the food prep that can be done in advance. Get the wine and beer on ice, and create any batch cocktails you're serving so they have time to chill. Once most of the food prep is done, I get my table or buffet or bar set up with any linens and flowers I might be using. I also do a few quick things to make cleaning up after the party a breeze, like emptying out the dishwasher, finding a laundry basket to collect table linens post-dinner, and taking the garbage and recycling out so that the bins are empty at the start of the party.

Right before the party starts I do my final run-through of the house. Fluff the pillows, put a fresh guest towel in the bathroom, fill the ice bucket with ice, and put out the first appetizers. Then, with just a moment to spare, it's time to put on some lipstick and pour yourself a drink! It's time to party.

Spring

SPRING GARDEN LUNCHEON MENU

Spring Vegetable Crudité Board

Garlic Herb Vegetable Dip

Mushroom, Asparagus, Pea, and Leek Risotto

Grilled Steak and Vegetable Kabobs
Marinated in Lemon and Rosemary

Grilled Peach and Arugula Salad
With Goat Cheese and a Balsamic Reduction

Lemon Shortbread Cookies

Ginger-Rosemary Lemonade
Made with a Ginger-Rosemary Simple Syrup

THE FIRST SIGNS OF SPRING IN NEW ENGLAND ALWAYS FEEL LIKE A CAUSE FOR CELEBRATION. I moved to Boston for college, and the first winter I spent in the city was a brutal one. I witnessed some epic snowstorms and truly understood the concept of hibernation for the first time in my life. I'll always remember though, more than that tough snowy winter, how the whole city came alive at the first signs of spring. It's as if everyone had been hiding (and really, we had been!) and suddenly opened up their doors to bask in the hints of warm sun and grass sprouting up through the melting snow. It is certainly a reason to celebrate, and there is camaraderie among New Englanders around the survival of the winter months. I have found that there is no better topic of conversation to embark on with familiar faces and strangers alike than the marvel of New England's changing seasons.

It's one of my favorite parts about living here. The dramatic change of seasons makes me appreciate each one more. As spring arrives, I always find a charge of energy to spend as much time as possible outdoors. Don't worry, I'm not talking about hiking; I'm more of a drinks-on-the-patio type of outdoorswoman. I may even go so far as to say I experience "spring guilt"—the terrible feeling when I waste a good-weather day inside, especially with those days of cabin fever still close by in the rearview mirror.

The first signs of spring weather are key in dictating how I plan a menu for entertaining this time of year, in the very same way I would plan my spring outfits. My heart says to get outside, break out the sundresses and sandals, and spread out the picnic blankets to bask in the sun. My head knows that spring in New England is fickle, and I should probably pack my quilted barn coat in my tote bag because the cool air

can often linger until June. Planning a menu works the same way. I'm ready to grab my market tote and scoop up all the bright green fresh vegetables and turn on the grill for the first time. At the same time the menu is best served with the balance of a few heartier elements to help ease out of the cooler months.

There is no surer sign of the change of the seasons than the opening of our local farmer's markets. It's an amazing time for fresh produce and to feel that energy of the warmer weather bringing the coastal New England region back to life. This time of year I look for bright salad greens, crisp stalks of asparagus, fresh sweet English peas, and big bunches of crunchy spring radishes. For that earthy, hearty balance, I also love to add mushrooms into my recipes. Bundles of fresh herbs are another springtime favorite; they bring so much color and flavor to a dish and taste so crisp after a long winter.

This spring garden luncheon menu takes inspiration from those ingredients, and a balance of fresh spring vegetables with some heartier dishes. The Mushroom, Asparagus, Pea, and Leek Risotto recipe is a perfect example of balancing the flavor scales at the change of the seasons. This dish is full of spring vegetables and sharp green pops of color, which play nicely with the warm earthy mushrooms and comfort-food depth of a creamy risotto. The ingredients blend together for a spoonful of flavors that are quintessentially spring.

My approach for spring entertaining is all about finding simple, unfussy ways to bring the party outdoors. Sometimes I'm so eager to get cooking and eating outside that we've hosted family for an outdoor spring meal before our patio furniture has even been brought outside and cleaned off. Forget the tablecloths and formal place settings and prioritize unpretentious and casual entertaining this time of year. It could be a few thick wool blankets spread across the fresh spring grass for a luncheon picnic, or a simple buffet on the patio. For decorations, the freshest of early spring flowers are your best bet. To keep with the casual theme, arrange them in small mason jars and send guests home with a bunch at the end of the meal.

My favorite way to entertain outdoors is with a menu that's easy to snack on. I start with a heaping crudité platter placed on one of our porch ottomans. The rest of the menu—grilled steak skewers, warm risotto, and a green salad—are all designed to be easy dishes for eating with a plate in your lap on the porch steps. Citrus-filled cocktails and an easy-to-grab dessert, like shortbread cookies, round out the laid-back menu and party experience.

BUILD A BEAUTIFUL SPRING VEGETABLE CRUDITÉ PLATTER

I learned something interesting while writing this book. Did you know that the term *crudité* means "rawness"? It's a term I've used countless times when preparing for a party, and I only recently discovered the name's origins. It is essentially a method of serving raw vegetables, but I know it to be so much more—it happens to be one of my favorite entertaining dishes. A crudité platter is almost always on my menu-plan for gatherings, big or small, because it's a wonderful way to add tons of color and flavor to a table. It's also a delicious and easy way to incorporate the bounty of seasonal vegetables available locally in the spring and summer—go and get inspired by what is fresh and in-season.

There are a few styling secrets that I rely on to build an eye-catching platter of vegetables that will wow your guests. Here is how to do it:

Build around Your Dips. Plan your crudité display on a large tray or board, and start with your dips. Place a few bowls or other small vessels for your dips on the tray and space them out evenly. You'll fill in the tray with your "dippables" among these bowls, so think about the negative space that is left around them.

Think Bite-Size. Prepare your veggies with snacking in mind. Guests will want to grab pieces off the plate to dunk into the cool dips and move on, so make it easy for them with bite-size pieces of vegetables. Slice larger radishes or cucumbers into thin discs, halve or quarter larger carrots, and trim down asparagus and green beans and celery into pieces that are easy to dip and nibble on.

Alternate Colors and Vary Textures. As you start to layer vegetables onto the platter, play with how the colors and textures of each ingredient look next to one another. Space out the green tones of asparagus, peppers, and broccoli by alternating them with the bright warm tones of tomatoes, and crisp radish slices. Consider the varied nature of textures and shapes, too, alternating round radishes and tomatoes with longer, thinner celery and carrot sticks.

Add Height. Add some vertical height to your crudité platter by standing up select veggies in small mason jars or shot glasses. Fresh string beans, trimmed asparagus, carrot sticks, or celery stalks all work well to add vertical height to the display.

Use Edible Containers. A creative way to house dips, hummus, or guacamole on a crudité board is with edible containers. Use a paring knife to slice off the top of a radicchio head. Then carefully hollow out the inside by sliding the knife into the head at an angle, removing the radicchio center to house your dip. An artichoke can make another interesting container for dips. Slice off the artichoke stem to give it a flat base, and then carefully remove the artichoke thorns, inner petals, choke, and heart and use it as a dip container. For a more modern look, endive leaves can hold individually spooned portions of dip on your crudité tray.

Finishing Touches. Nestle in bowls of pickles, olives, or rustic crackers to balance out the crisp flavors of the vegetables. Finish the plate with a sprinkle of fresh-cut herbs over the dips for a pop of green and additional texture.

Tip

For a beautiful presentation of your grilled steak kabobs, fill a large platter with a bed of fresh greens, like arugula. Nestle the kabobs on the greens after they've had a chance to cool for a few minutes. Add an additional touch of rosemary to the dish by removing the needles from the bottom half of a rosemary sprig. Tuck the bottom half of the sprig into the top of the kabob, threading it along the hole where the skewer enters the veggies.

Grilled Peach and Arugula Salad

With Goat Cheese and a Balsamic Reduction

SERVES 6

When putting together a menu for a luncheon or a dinner party, I often feel bad for the poor salad on the list—it gets penciled in with the thought: Oh, I guess we should have a salad, too. The salad can come as an afterthought to the main course, but it doesn't have to! Fresh arugula greens are typically one of the first items we see at our spring farmer's market, and they make a great base for this salad. The rich, creamy crumbles of locally made goat cheese shine against the peppery flavors of arugula. To balance these flavors out, I lean on the heat of the grill to bring out the sugars in juicy stone fruit, like peaches. Bold, caramelized and charred grill marks on the fruit look so very appetizing tossed into the bowl. The whole thing is finished off with a drizzle of thickened balsamic vinegar and mashed peaches—both tart and sweet from reducing on the stovetop. A few simple ingredients combine together for a salad that will never feel like an afterthought.

INGREDIENTS

6 large firm peaches

Olive oil

¾ cup balsamic vinegar

Arugula

4 ounces goat cheese

Freshly cracked black pepper

INSTRUCTIONS

Preheat grill to medium-high heat.

While the grill is warming up, prepare your peaches. Halve peaches along their seams and remove the pit. Drizzle lightly with olive oil.

Place peach halves on the grill and cook for about 4–5 minutes on each side, until charred grill marks appear and the sugars begin to caramelize.

Remove peaches from the grill; reserve five peaches for the salad.

Take the remaining peach and remove the skin. Mash the softened interior in a small saucepan and combine with balsamic vinegar.

Cook the peach and balsamic mixture over medium heat for about 10–15 minutes, until it is reduced by more than half and thickens. Remove from heat and let cool slightly.

Fill a large bowl with washed arugula leaves, nestle in the grilled peaches, and top with goat cheese crumbles. Season lightly with freshly cracked black pepper and drizzle the balsamic-peach reduction over the salad before serving.

Tip

Peaches are the fruit of choice in this version, and get their fame from southern states like Georgia, but actually grow well in southern New England too. If peaches aren't available though, consider swapping in another stone fruit like tart plums or sweet apricots. Similarly, you can experiment with combinations of other soft cheeses paired with the fruit and arugula—like Gorgonzola—if goat cheese isn't your thing.

Lemon Shortbread Cookies

SERVES 24

I'm much more of a cook than a baker, but even the most hurried baker can throw these shortbread cookies together with little effort. To give the shortbread an update for spring, I work in fresh lemon juice and zest—the citrus brightens up the sweet and buttery flavors; add a little extra zest on top before serving. These cookies pair perfectly with a cup of tea at the end of a luncheon.

This recipe also makes a fun, buttery, sticky dough and is a great way to get kids involved in the kitchen—have them help shape the dough into a ball and roll it out before you stamp out the cookies with cookie cutters. Plus it's egg-free, so it's totally fine to sneak a little bite of cookie dough while you're working with it!

INGREDIENTS

2 tablespoons fresh lemon juice

2 tablespoons fresh lemon zest

2 cups (4 sticks) butter, softened

1 cup granulated sugar

4 cups flour

INSTRUCTIONS

Preheat oven to 350°F. Line a baking sheet with parchment paper.

Combine fresh lemon juice, lemon zest, butter, and sugar in a bowl. Beat with a hand mixer until light and fluffy.

Sift flour into the butter mixture and stir to fully combine the ingredients.

Use your hands to pack the dough together into two balls, cover in plastic wrap, and refrigerate for 20 minutes.

After the dough chills, place it on a floured work surface and use a rolling pin to roll out the dough to ½ inch thickness.

Stamp the dough with your desired cookie-cutter shape and transfer to baking sheet.

Bake the cookies at 350°F for 11–12 minutes, watching the color of the cookies closely, until they just start to turn a light golden color.

Remove the cookies from the oven and let them rest for 2–3 minutes before transferring to a wire cooling rack to cool completely.

Tip

This cookie dough lends itself well to being shaped with cookie cutters. I've used alphabet cookie cutters to stamp out guests' initials for edible place cards set at each place setting. Get creative with your cookie shapes to match the season or the event.

Ginger-Rosemary Lemonade
Made with a Ginger-Rosemary Simple Syrup
SERVES 6-8

When hosting a luncheon, I tend to assume that the cocktail drinking will be a bit lighter than at an evening event. One way that I plan for a balance of alcoholic and non-alcoholic drinks is by making a signature drink that can be easily served on its own, or "spiked" for my friends and family who are looking for something a bit stronger. For this spring menu I serve a ginger-rosemary lemonade that is absolutely delicious as a stand-alone drink. Use high-quality lemonade and serve it with homemade ginger-rosemary syrup. Glasses will look festive with lemon slices and rosemary sprigs adorning their rims. The drink also blends well with a variety of hard alcohols. Mix in a splash of gin for more of the pine notes found in the rosemary, or stir in vodka to let the ginger and lemon flavors shine.

INGREDIENTS

1 cup granulated sugar

1 cup water

3 tablespoons peeled and diced fresh ginger

3 rosemary sprigs

Ice

Lemonade

Vodka or gin, optional

INSTRUCTIONS

In a small saucepan, combine sugar, water, ginger, and rosemary. Simmer over medium-low heat until reduced by half.

Remove any ginger or rosemary pieces and strain syrup into a glass container; cool syrup to room temperature before using.

Fill a glass with ice and pour 1 to 2 tablespoons of the ginger-rosemary syrup over the top. Top with lemonade and stir to combine.

Optional: Add 1.5 ounces of gin or vodka to the glass before topping with lemonade and stirring.

EASTER EGG HUNT BRUNCH MENU

Orange Poppy Seed Mini Donuts

Homemade Honey Almond Granola
With Blackberry and Yogurt Parfaits

Deviled Eggs with Chives

Baked Breakfast Strata
With Italian Sausage and Goat Cheese

Cheddar Scallion Hash Browns

Crispy Bacon
With a Maple Brown Sugar Glaze

Easter Brunch Mimosas
Juices, Champagne, and Garnishes

BRUNCH. It's one of my favorite food words, and certainly one of my favorite meals. It brings connotations of relaxing weekends, indulgent and comforting breakfast foods, and an always-excellent excuse to start pouring cocktails before noon. When I started writing this chapter, I did what any good writer does: procrastinate for a bit by digging deep into a rabbit hole of Internet research. It turned out my time was not wasted though, because in my scrolling and reading I came upon some interesting facts about this beloved late-morning mealtime. What I learned was that brunch first gained mainstream popularity in the 1940s as a way to celebrate and share a meal with family immediately following church services, particularly on Easter Sunday. I relished for a bit in this newfound brunch knowledge—that I will no doubt drop into conversation the next time my girlfriends and I are sipping mimosas together—because my own history with this meal is deeply rooted in early memories of Easter brunch celebrations.

As a child I spent every Easter Sunday getting dressed up in my finest floral-patterned dress to attend Easter church services with my extended family. I patiently sat through the singing and sermons with my eye on the prize: skipping my shiny little Mary Janes over to the annual Easter egg hunt and brunch thrown by my grandparents' close friends.

The Easter egg hunt itself was a big draw for the dozens of kids at the party. We lined up with Easter baskets that were nearly as large as our little bodies and took off sprinting into the yard to find the hand-dyed pastel treasures. We hunted and hoped we'd uncover the few special plastic eggs filled with shiny nickels and quarters. My strategy was always to snake around to the front of the house to check for eggs in the flowerbeds and inside the mailbox. It was a foolproof way to snag a few eggs and then loop right back through the front door where the Easter buffet was laid out for everyone to feast on.

As an adult who eats, sleeps, thinks, and writes about food, I can attest that my food memories of this Easter brunch have been a huge influence on how I entertain and cook today. The things that stick out to me in my memories of these brunches are so very sensory: the warm steam coming off piping-hot fluffy scrambled eggs, the bright pinky-orange colors of thinly sliced lox topped with capers, and the incredible scent of brown sugar–glazed bacon wafting through the house as the oven door opened. A variation of that very same bacon is in this chapter; it is a mainstay in my brunch-menu arsenal. When I host a party now, I often think back to how all those elements came together at this famed Easter brunch to make my family and the other guests feel so welcome and at home.

The kids who waited at that Easter egg hunt starting line have all grown up now, and many of us have families of our own. As it goes, our traditions evolve and we start new ones. These days we spend Easter at my in-laws house, and I've loved experiencing and learning from their food traditions. My mother-in-law makes picture-perfect deviled eggs as an appetizer at their Easter celebrations, which I've now adopted as one of my favorite brunch-menu additions. We also participated in a "grown-up" Easter egg hunt last year. My creative mother-in-law wrote dozens of riddles as clues to find Easter eggs filled with candy and coffee shop gift cards—everyone was a kid again! A perfect example of how much fun it can be to start new traditions.

NEW TRADITIONS FOR EASTER BRUNCH

Brunch comes with a tightly curated selection of menu mainstays: bacon, eggs, pancakes, pastries, coffees, and juices. There is comfort in these items because they're so familiar to us. It's fun to experiment and add new traditions to shake up your brunch rituals and surprise your guests.

Build a Bagel Bar. I've lived in New England for almost half my life now, but by birth I am a New Yorker, and my love for bagels runs deep. One of my favorite casual brunch ideas is to set up a DIY bagel bar. Pair a large basket of pre-sliced bagels in several varieties with a tray of bagel spreads and toppings. Offer a plain cream cheese, a veggie or herb cream cheese, and one sweet option too, like maple walnut. Lox, capers, thinly sliced red onions and cucumbers, fresh herbs, micro greens, or berries are all delicious topping options. A bagel sandwich bar is another unique spin on this concept. Serve a tray of crispy bacon and hash browns, various cheeses, and warm scrambled eggs alongside toasted bagels for a DIY breakfast sandwich bar.

French Toast Twist. I'm firmly a savory-brunch person, always opting for the rich eggs Benedict over a sweet stack of pancakes or french toast. I always look longingly, though, at my brunch-mates' restaurant order and wish I could have just one bite of their sweet selection. My solution for this problem is to create a savory-style french toast by whisking in fresh herbs and a dash of mustard to the standard egg and milk french toast batter. Serve them warm and topped with fried eggs and a sprinkle of a sharp cheese like cheddar or Parmesan. It's the best of both worlds.

Bite-Size Stacks. I'm a firm believer that things always taste better and look cuter when they're served in mini form. For this brunch menu, I've experimented with mini donuts and served mini parfaits in individual glass containers. Another crowd-pleasing dish that is easy to shrink down into bite-size stacks are pancakes. Mix up a batch of your favorite pancake batter and drop two-inch circles onto a hot griddle. Serve them stacked four to five pancakes high with a festive toothpick flag to hold the bites together. They make a delicious and eye-catching appetizer at any holiday brunch.

The elements of this Easter menu translate well to any brunch-time occasion. These dishes work for birthdays, baby and bridal showers, or just a good reason to get your friends together. In fact, as parents of a young daughter, we find our most enjoyable way to entertain these days is during the daytime on the weekends. Kids are well rested and can easily play during brunch-time hours, and many of the menu staples are inherently kid-friendly. Plus when your kids get you up at 5 a.m., mom and dad are ready for a mimosa at 11 a.m.

Almost all these recipes are easily transportable too. Bring the strata dish to a family potluck party, or pack up the parfaits, deviled eggs, and mini donuts in containers and head to the park for a picnic brunch!

Orange Poppy Seed Mini Donuts

SERVES 12

I try to avoid "specialty" cookware. I hate clutter and am pressed for space in a small but workable kitchen. I also know the frustration of reading a recipe and finding out that I need to head to the store to purchase a fancy new pan before I've even gotten my measuring spoons dirty. This recipe, though, is one that I've made an exception for, and I hope you will too. Hop online right now and purchase a mini donut baking pan. It will be the most wonderful $10 you've ever spent, because now you can make mini donuts every weekend and impress your friends and family and coworkers with tiny sweet breakfast treats. This recipe for orange poppy seed mini donuts is an Easter brunch–inspired twist. They're best served warm while the sweet glaze is still fresh and sticky. If you plan to make them in advance of a party, wait to glaze them until right before you plate them for the best flavor and presentation.

INGREDIENTS

For Donuts

Nonstick cooking spray

2½ tablespoons butter, melted and cooled

⅓ cup whole milk

1 teaspoon vanilla extract

1½ tablespoons orange juice

1 egg

¼ cup granulated sugar

1 cup flour

1 teaspoon baking powder

¼ teaspoon salt

½ tablespoon orange zest

Poppy seeds

For Glaze

¼ cup orange juice

1 teaspoon orange zest

1 tablespoon honey (orange blossom honey is best!)

1 cup confectioners' sugar

INSTRUCTIONS

Preheat oven to 400°F. Prepare a twelve-cavity mini donut pan by coating the interior with nonstick cooking spray.

In a large bowl, combine melted butter, milk, vanilla, and orange juice. Whisk in egg and sugar until just combined.

Sift together flour, baking powder, and salt. Fold dry ingredients and orange zest into wet ingredient mixture until combined, being careful not to overmix.

Transfer donut batter into a pastry bag (a plastic sandwich bag with one corner snipped open will work too). Pipe about half the batter into the twelve mini donut pan cavities, so that each one is three-quarters full.

Bake at 400°F for 5 minutes. Remove the pan from the oven and carefully flip each donut using a fork, then return to the oven. Bake for an additional 3 minutes before removing from the oven and letting the donuts cool slightly before transferring to a wire cooling rack.

While donuts are baking, prepare the glaze. Combine orange juice, orange zest, honey, and confectioners' sugar with a whisk.

Dip each warm donut into the orange glaze and then sprinkle with poppy seeds; serve immediately.

Homemade Honey Almond Granola
With Blackberry and Yogurt Parfaits
SERVES 8

I've hosted about twenty-seven baby and bridal showers in my life. It turns out that when you write a food and entertaining blog, you move pretty high up the list as a potential shower hostess. I joke, but I love any great reason to celebrate with friends, family, and brunch! These parfaits in small mason jars look absolutely darling on a shower buffet table and always feel like a healthy option for guests who might not want to eat bacon, croissants, and rich, cheesy quiches (I'm not sure who those people are, but I hear they exist). This variation for our Easter brunch combines tart blackberries with a homemade honey almond granola. For an extra-special touch, flavor the plain Greek yogurt with a bit of orange zest and honey to pick up on the other sweet and citrus notes on the brunch menu.

INGREDIENTS

For Granola
1½ cups rolled oats
½ cup sliced almonds
2 tablespoons vegetable oil
1 tablespoon brown sugar
3 tablespoons honey
1 teaspoon vanilla extract

For Parfaits
Granola
4 cups plain Greek yogurt
2 tablespoons honey
1 tablespoon orange zest
2 cups blackberries

INSTRUCTIONS
Preheat oven to 350°F.

In a large bowl, combine rolled oats, sliced almonds, vegetable oil, brown sugar, honey, and vanilla.

Stir ingredients thoroughly and spread out in a single layer on a rimmed baking sheet.

Bake at 350°F for 20 minutes, stirring midway through the bake time.

Remove the granola from the oven and let cool completely.

Flavor the Greek yogurt with honey and orange zest and stir to fully incorporate the ingredients.

Assemble the parfaits by dividing yogurt into eight small mason jars, about ½ cup in each. Top with blackberries and finish with a scoop of cooled granola.

Tip

When it comes to building a parfait, simply stick to the yogurt-fruit-granola trifecta. Play with different combinations of fruits and berries, mix in flavored or regular Greek yogurts, and add in textural elements like nuts or seeds. These parfaits also pack up nicely in their individual mason jar containers for brunch on the go!

Deviled Eggs with Chives

SERVES 8

Deviled eggs have a tradition as an appetizer and can often be spotted on summer barbecue menus too. I came to add them to brunch menus, though, as an easy way to incorporate eggs into the meal without having to stand over the stove during a party to churn out hot scrambled or fried eggs to my guests. They are a perfect brunch dish to prep the night before guests arrive. My fondness for these bite-size eggs is well known among my family members; when they hit the table at gatherings, my husband knows to alert me so that I can quickly make my way to the deviled egg plate before they disappear.

INGREDIENTS

10 large eggs
½ cup mayonnaise
1 teaspoon spicy brown mustard
½ teaspoon paprika
¼ teaspoon salt
½ teaspoon black pepper
Minced fresh chives, for garnish

INSTRUCTIONS

Place eggs in a single layer in a saucepan and cover with cold water. Heat on high until water begins to boil. Once the water boils for about 2–3 minutes, cover, and remove from heat.

Let the covered pot sit for about 15 minutes before removing the eggs and rinsing under cold water.

Carefully crack and peel the eggshells, then run under cool water to remove any shell remnants.

Slice the shelled eggs in half lengthwise and remove and transfer yolks to a bowl. Place the egg white halves on a serving platter.

Mash the egg yolks and stir in mayonnaise, mustard, paprika, salt, and pepper.

Evenly spoon the yolk mixture back into the egg whites and garnish with minced fresh chives and additional cracked black pepper.

Chill at least 20 minutes before serving.

Baked Breakfast Strata
With Italian Sausage and Goat Cheese
SERVES 6-8

In every holiday menu, especially if we're entertaining during the morning, I try to add a few dishes to the mix that can be prepared the night before. It makes getting ready for a party a far more enjoyable experience when all your prep-work tools are already washed and put away. I love when you can just slide a dish into the oven while you fix your makeup and welcome your guests. This baked breakfast strata is one of those make-ahead recipes that my family always relies on when we're celebrating a holiday with a brunch-time gathering.

Another perk of this recipe is that it uses up day-old bread that's gotten a bit dried out. The egg and milk mixture absorbs overnight for a fluffy, savory, french toast–textured casserole, reviving the crusty bread pieces.

INGREDIENTS

1 large loaf day-old French bread (about 8 cups cubed)

10 eggs

½ cup whole milk

Salt and black pepper

½ cup homemade pesto, plus 2–3 tablespoons for the top

1½ cups cooked crumbled Italian sausage

½ cup crumbled goat cheese, plus 2–3 tablespoons for the top

INSTRUCTIONS

Cube bread into 1-inch-square pieces and arrange in a baking dish.

In a bowl, whisk together eggs and milk until combined and season with salt and pepper.

Pour the egg mixture evenly over the cubed bread and lightly toss the pieces together so that each piece is coated. Add pesto and continue to toss to evenly distribute on the bread pieces.

Fold in cooked Italian sausage pieces and crumbled goat cheese, pressing the entire mixture down into the baking dish.

Top the dish with reserved pesto and goat cheese. Cover the dish with plastic wrap and refrigerate at least 2 hours or overnight.

When ready to bake, preheat oven to 375°F. Remove plastic wrap and bake for 45 minutes. Serve warm.

Note: Before you place the dish in the oven, check to see how the eggs and milk have absorbed into the bread. You want the mixture to be absorbed, but still look moist and spongy. If the bread looks dried out, whisk together one additional egg and 2 tablespoons milk and pour over the top before placing in the oven.

Tip

Experiment with different "mix-ins" to give the dish a range of flavor combinations. Chop up sun-dried tomatoes and mix them into this version of the recipe, or replace the Italian sausage and goat cheese with a sweet breakfast sausage and gruyère cheese. For an extra-savory spin, try crispy bacon pieces, sharp cheddar cheese, and minced scallions mixed into the bread and egg base.

Cheddar Scallion Hash Browns

SERVES 6

I'd like to dedicate this recipe to my brother and sister, who are experts in the hash brown department. They take their job very seriously and taste-test crispy hash browns with precision at diners and delis, leaving no savory potato bite behind. I'm a fan of the hash brown too, and have a similar love of the crispy potatoes tucked into layers of a warm breakfast sandwich. I wanted to find a way to bring the diner-inspired dish into a brunch menu that's a bit more refined, and came up with a version that mixes in the sharp flavors of scallions and cheddar cheese.

It is totally fine to use frozen shredded potatoes to make quick work of this recipe. Let the potatoes thaw in a bowl for about fifteen to twenty minutes before cooking, and pat dry any excess moisture to help them crisp. If you have the time to work with fresh potatoes, choose russet potatoes, shred them in a bowl, and par-cook in the microwave for two to three minutes; remove any excess liquid before mixing with the other ingredients. Use good-quality cheddar in this recipe and you'll notice a difference in the taste—the sharpness will come through in the final result.

I always want more of these potatoes, and having leftovers is a great excuse to make a breakfast sandwich the morning after the party. If you double the recipe, make sure to cook the potatoes in multiple batches so the pan doesn't become overcrowded. A thin layer of potatoes in the pan will ensure they cook evenly and get the crispy texture you're looking for.

INGREDIENTS

1 egg

4 cups shredded potatoes

1 cup shredded sharp cheddar cheese

½ cup minced fresh scallions

1 teaspoon paprika

¼ teaspoon garlic powder

¼ teaspoon onion powder

Salt and black pepper

INSTRUCTIONS

In a large bowl, whisk egg and fold in shredded potatoes, cheddar cheese, and fresh scallions.

Season potato mixture with paprika, garlic powder, onion powder, salt, and pepper; stir to fully combine.

Heat a griddle or large cast-iron skillet over medium-high heat; coat the pan with cooking spray.

Working in batches to avoid crowding the pan, add half the potato mixture onto the heated surface and evenly distribute. Let the potatoes heat in the pan undisturbed until they begin to crisp and stick together.

Use a large spatula to flip the potatoes and crisp the other side.

Remove from pan after both sides are fully cooked and crisped, about 7–10 minutes.

Repeat with remaining batches of potatoes. Serve hot and garnish with additional fresh scallions.

Crispy Bacon
With a Maple Brown Sugar Glaze
SERVES 6-8

I have a very distinct scent-memory from my childhood at Easter brunches of crispy glazed bacon wafting out of the kitchen. It was at these brunches that I learned the art of befriending the chef; if you hang around the kitchen you'll be first in line to snag a piece of the delicious sweet, crispy bacon that has just come out of the oven. Our family friend that hosted these brunches is rather famous for her glazed bacon, and I've tried to re-create it at home dozens of times. Like most family recipes, it'll never taste quite like the perfect memory of the original version. I like to think I've gotten close, and I've had the wonderful experience of filling my own house with that warm, sugary bacon scent as I tested it.

INGREDIENTS
1 pound bacon
1 tablespoon maple syrup
1½ tablespoons brown sugar

INSTRUCTIONS
Preheat oven to 375°F.

On a large rimmed baking sheet, arrange the bacon slices in a single layer. Bake at 375°F for 30 minutes.

Remove the bacon from the oven. Drizzle bacon with maple syrup and sprinkle brown sugar on top. Use the back of a spoon to spread the syrup and brown sugar evenly across each piece.

Return to the oven for an additional 5 minutes, until the syrup and sugar caramelize on the crispy bacon slices.

EASTER BRUNCH MIMOSAS

I think we can all agree on one thing: It's not brunch without mimosas. The festive bubbly drinks go hand-in-hand with the very act of brunching and are a key element on your brunch menu. The recipe for a mimosa is fairly simple: Fill a flute halfway with chilled champagne and top the remaining half of the glass with orange juice. It doesn't get easier than that! Even though the recipe is about as basic as they come, there are still plenty of ways to make your Easter brunch mimosa bar feel elevated and special.

Use Real Glassware. I think a case of champagne glasses is one of the best things you can have on hand for entertaining. A real glass champagne flute makes everyone feel festive, and you can find relatively affordable "caterers"-style sets that aren't a huge investment. If you don't think you're ready to spring for your own set of champagne flutes, rent a case of them from a party supply company. The best part of renting glassware is that you can return them unwashed, which cuts down on post-party cleanup time!

Display Juices. For a mimosa bar, I like to have a few containers of orange juice on hand and then another one or two juices for other drink combinations. A peach juice for bellinis and a tart grapefruit juice are typically my favorite options in the mimosa bar rotation. Make sure all the juices are chilled before guests arrive. When you're ready to set out the mixers, pour them into labeled clear carafes for display.

Bring the Bubbles. Chilled champagne is the key element to a mimosa; plan to get about six to eight drinks out of a standard 750 ml bottle. Prosecco or Cava are great affordable alternatives for your mimosa bar; choose something dry and not too sweet to balance the natural sugar in the juices. I also like to add a non-alcoholic bottle of something bubbly to the bar for guests as another option, like a sparkling water or cider.

Finish with Garnishes. To make a festive cocktail even more celebration-worthy, add a few fun garnishes to the table for guests to add to their DIY drinks. Bowls of freshly sliced fruits and berries, pieces of candied ginger, or flavored liqueurs with citrus or herbal notes are a few options. You can also match the color scheme of your party with fun straws or drink stirrers to create eye-catching drinks and add interest to your mimosa bar.

FARMER'S MARKET DINNER PARTY MENU

English Pea Hummus
Served with Radishes and Pita Spears

Crispy Crab Cakes
And Old Bay Aioli

Farmer's Market Pasta

Carrot Ribbon Salad
With a Simple Vinaigrette

Seared Scallops
In Lemon Brown Butter Sauce

Elderflower Aperol Fizz

I'M A FARMER'S MARKET JUNKIE. Some women like to weave their way through the shoe displays at department stores, ogling the fancy footwear with coveting glances. I take that very same wide-eyed approach as I stroll through an open-air farmer's market. Instead of pining for a pair of Louboutins, I lust for mile-high displays of colorful pink and purple radishes.

My local market is idyllic, overlooking the ocean. It's the nicest way to spend a Saturday morning, pushing my daughter in her stroller around the market, breathing in the salt air as I shop. This market is much more than just a spot for local produce; there are farms selling fresh cuts of meat, local cheeses, and dairy products, and fishermen with fresh seafood that could have been caught yards away from the beach parking lot we're standing in. There are bakeries with warm bread that smells like heaven, a woman that sells homemade pies (sweet and savory!), and producers of local honeys, hot sauces, granolas, and snacks. For a food-nerd like me, it's more than just grocery shopping; it's a place to be inspired.

One of my favorite entertaining ideas when we are hosting family for the weekend is to make a trip to the market together to plan our dinner menu. We take a full loop of the market booths and scan the displays for inspiration. Then we discuss what looked good, usually over a frozen lemonade and baked treat from the vendors, and make our plan. It's a fun activity to do with our houseguests, a bit of communal menu planning so that everyone is part of the meal. That is exactly how this springtime menu came to be, from a morning at the farmer's market with my family, where we plucked the best vegetables and seafood and fresh pasta and herbs from the stands to cook together.

English Pea Hummus
Served with Radishes and Pita Spears
SERVES 6-8

When I see fresh peas at the market, I can't resist working them into a recipe. They're especially delicious in pasta recipes. I also make them as a side dish with a simple finish of butter, salt, and pepper.

Fresh English peas give this hummus tons of flavor and a bright green color. I have been able to find them at my specialty grocery store already shelled, which makes for quick work of this dish. If you find them at your farmer's market, pick out firm, bright, heavy pods and plan to purchase about one and a half pounds for this recipe, which should equate to around one and a half cups of shelled peas.

This dip gets added flavor from garlic, tahini, and spices and herbs like cumin, red pepper, and parsley. Serve it with a swirl of good olive oil on top, crispy radish slices, and fluffy pita bread toasts.

INGREDIENTS

1½ cups fresh English peas
2 large garlic cloves, peeled
¼ cup olive oil, plus more for serving
¼ cup tahini
2 tablespoons lemon juice
1 tablespoon Parmesan cheese
1 tablespoon fresh parsley
½ teaspoon cumin
¼ teaspoon red pepper flakes
Salt and black pepper
Radishes, sliced, for serving
Pita bread, for serving

INSTRUCTIONS

Bring a pot of salted water to a boil and add peas; cook for 3–4 minutes, until the peas are tender. Drain the peas and run under cold water in a colander. Pat peas dry with a paper towel.

Add the cooked and dried peas, peeled garlic cloves, olive oil, tahini, fresh lemon juice, Parmesan, fresh parsley leaves, cumin, and red pepper flakes to a food processor; blend the ingredients together until smooth.

Taste and season with salt and pepper, then transfer to a bowl for serving and swirl a drizzle of olive oil on top. Serve with thinly sliced fresh radishes and spears of lightly toasted pita bread.

Crispy Crab Cakes
And Old Bay Aioli
SERVES 5

Crab cakes are surprisingly easy to make at home. For restaurant-level delicious-ness, first secure quality ingredients. Fresh crabmeat has the best flavor, but Jumbo or Lump canned crabmeat will work too. Fresh veggies give the crab cake some texture, and the Dijon mustard, Worcestershire sauce, and hot sauce amp up the flavor. Chill cakes for about thirty minutes before cooking to help retain shape and structure in the skillet.

INGREDIENTS

2 cups Lump crabmeat (about ¾ pound)

¾ cup panko bread crumbs

½ cup shredded and minced carrots

¼ cup finely minced red bell pepper

2 tablespoons minced fresh parsley

2 tablespoons minced scallions

1 large egg

⅓ cup mayonnaise

1 teaspoon Dijon mustard

1 teaspoon Worcestershire sauce

6–8 dashes of Tabasco sauce

Salt and black pepper

Olive oil

Arugula, lemon wedges, and Old Bay Aioli, for serving

For the Old Bay Aioli

1 cup mayonnaise

1 tablespoon fresh lemon juice

1 teaspoon minced fresh parsley

¼ teaspoon Tabasco sauce

¼ teaspoon Old Bay Seasoning

Black pepper

INSTRUCTIONS

In a large bowl, combine crabmeat, bread crumbs, finely minced carrots, red bell pepper, parsley, and scallions. Toss lightly to combine.

In a separate bowl, whisk the egg with the remaining wet ingredients: mayo, Dijon, Worcestershire, and Tabasco sauce.

With a fork, fold the wet ingredients into the crab mixture, fluffing the ingredients together until just incorporated. Season with salt and pepper.

Scoop out ½-cup portions of the crab mixture and loosely pack into balls. Set the crab balls onto a parchment paper–lined baking sheet and press them down to form the crab-cake-patty shape. Repeat to create five uniformly shaped crab cakes.

Chill the crab cakes for 30 minutes in the refrigerator to firm up their shape and structure.

Meanwhile, for the aioli, combine mayonnaise, fresh lemon juice, minced parsley, Tabasco sauce, and Old Bay Seasoning in a bowl. Taste and season with cracked black pepper. Chill for at least 30 minutes.

Heat a drizzle of olive oil over medium-high heat in a large skillet and add the crab cakes to the pan when hot. Cook for about 6–8 minutes on each side, until crispy golden brown and cooked through.

Serve over a bed of arugula with fresh lemon wedges and homemade Old Bay Aioli.

Tip

These crab cakes can be prepared ahead of time and easily reheated in the oven before serving. Place the cooked crab cakes on a parchment-lined baking sheet and heat in the oven at 350°F for about 20 minutes to warm them through.

Farmer's Market Pasta

SERVES 6

The very best way to get me to eat vegetables is to toss them in butter and fold them into a big bowl of pasta. Fresh pasta is always better. I get it at the farmer's market, at the fresh pasta shop near my parents' house (they call and take our order before they come up to visit!), or make my own if I'm feeling up for the task.

The fresh pasta gets coated in a simple sauce made of shallots, butter, lemon, and white wine, and then is dressed with all the fresh vegetables I can find. This version uses peas, carrots, corn, and yellow summer squash, but I change it up each time I make it based on what I'm seeing at the market. I've made this same recipe with blanched broccolini, sautéed mushrooms, and slices of zucchini. There's an endless amount of combinations you could create; just let what is fresh and seasonal inspire you!

INGREDIENTS

1 pound fresh pasta (linguine or fettuccini)

1 cup fresh English peas

2 large carrots

1 ear of corn

1 yellow summer squash

1 large shallot

4 tablespoons (½ stick) butter

1 lemon

¼ cup white wine

¼ cup reserved pasta water

¼ cup Parmesan cheese

Salt and black pepper

INSTRUCTIONS

Bring a pot of salted water to a boil; cook the fresh pasta to al dente. Add the peas to the boiling water about 2 minutes before the pasta is finished cooking. Reserve about ¼ cup of the pasta cooking water before draining and setting the pasta and peas aside.

Use a vegetable peeler to cut the carrots into long ribbons; shuck corn and cut kernels off the corncob; thinly slice the yellow summer squash; and peel and thinly slice the shallot.

In a large pan, melt the butter over medium-high heat and sauté the shallots until they begin to soften. Add the carrots, corn, and yellow summer squash to the pan and sauté 5 minutes more.

Juice and zest the lemon, adding the liquid and zest to the pan. Add the white wine to deglaze the hot pan; scrape up any bits from the bottom of the pan.

Add the pasta, peas, and half of the reserved pasta water to the pan, tossing all the ingredients to combine and coat the pasta. Add more pasta water if needed.

Fold in the Parmesan cheese and season with salt and pepper to taste before serving.

Carrot Ribbon Salad

With a Simple Vinaigrette

SERVES 6

The item that most frequently gets tossed in the compost pile after a party is a green salad. There are a few salads in this book that I've had success with, but mostly because they're filled with lots of cheese and other delicious toppings. Hiding leafy greens under cheese is one of my favorite ways to trick people (me) into eating a salad. To limit waste, I've brainstormed some green salad alternatives to add to my entertaining menus. This carrot ribbon salad is one of my success stories in that category.

I make this salad often when hosting shower luncheons because it's so colorful and flavorful, and the taste continues to develop as the dressing marinates the raw vegetables. It's a great make-ahead dish for entertaining. The ribbons are long, thin peeled slices of raw carrots, which present beautifully with radishes and arugula and chopped walnuts tangled among the orange in a big serving bowl.

INGREDIENTS

12 medium-size carrots

2 cups arugula

1 cup thinly sliced radishes

½ cup walnuts

¼ cup olive oil

¼ cup apple cider vinegar

1 tablespoon grainy mustard

1 tablespoon honey

1½ teaspoons lemon juice

Salt and black pepper

INSTRUCTIONS

Use a vegetable peeler to remove and discard the skin of the carrots. Run the vegetable peeler down the length of the cleaned carrots, shaving off long ribbons until you have about 8 cups carrots in a large bowl.

Clean and roughly chop the arugula. Add arugula and sliced radishes to the bowl of carrot ribbons.

Roughly chop the walnuts and toast them on a baking sheet in a 350°F oven for 5–7 minutes; remove from oven and add to the bowl of carrots.

While the walnuts are toasting, prepare the salad dressing. Combine olive oil, vinegar, a grainy mustard, honey, and lemon juice in a small jar and vigorously shake until the oil and vinegar have emulsified.

Toss the vegetable and nut mixture with about two-thirds of the dressing, season with salt and pepper, and set aside in the fridge for at least 30 minutes to marinate.

Give the salad a toss before serving; add the remaining one-third reserved dressing if needed.

Seared Scallops
In Lemon Brown Butter Sauce
SERVES 6

Brown butter always lures me in on a dinner menu. Whatever it is that's under the brown butter is fine with me, just as long as it's a vehicle for that sweet, caramelized glaze. It works for other people too. It's not just me—it's actually how I got my sister to try scallops for the very first time.

To get the best results, pat the scallops dry before adding them to the pan to remove any moisture, and use a fairly high heat to get good browning on the outside. The delicious golden caramelized layer that forms on the scallops is what makes them so tasty. To make sure those scallops were as appealing as possible to a first-timer, I leaned on that beloved brown butter cooked with some white wine and lemon for a finishing sauce.

INGREDIENTS

1 pound large sea scallops

Salt and black pepper

4 tablespoons (½ stick) butter

2 tablespoons white wine

1 lemon

1 tablespoon chopped fresh parsley

INSTRUCTIONS

Pat scallops dry with a paper towel. If they still have a small side muscle attached, remove it by gently pulling it off the scallop body. Lightly season both sides of the scallops with salt and pepper.

Heat a large cast-iron or stainless steel skillet over medium-high heat and add butter to the hot pan. Cook the butter until it begins to change to a golden brown color and a light foam develops on the butter's surface.

Add the scallops to the hot pan with browned butter, being careful not to crowd the pan. Let the scallops sear and brown for about 3 minutes before flipping and cooking the other side. Spoon the brown butter over the scallops as they cook to baste them in the sauce.

Remove the scallops from the pan and set on a serving plate. Add the wine and juice of one lemon to the brown butter and allow the alcohol to deglaze the pan, cooking for another 2–3 minutes.

Pour the lemon brown butter sauce over the scallops and garnish with freshly chopped parsley before serving. Season with additional cracked black pepper to taste.

Elderflower Aperol Fizz

SERVES 1

This springtime farmer's market–inspired menu is all about highlighting bright, fresh flavors. A refreshing cocktail that can be sipped out on the grass as dinner gets plated for some patio dining is just what the menu needs to feel complete. One of my favorite refreshing cocktail ingredients is an elderflower liqueur. The floral aromas and honey-like sweetness of elderflower are a favorite way to dress up a glass of chilled prosecco.

This recipe combines that simple elderflower and champagne combination with aperol—which adds color, bitterness, and citrus to balance the flavors in the drink. Serve it in casual glassware with a big, zesty orange peel for added flavor on the rim of the glass!

INGREDIENTS

¾ **ounce elderflower liqueur**
½ **ounce aperol**
½ **ounce lemon juice**
Chilled champagne or prosecco
Orange peel, for garnish

INSTRUCTIONS

In a cocktail shaker, combine elderflower liqueur, aperol, and lemon juice over ice.

Shake and pour into a glass and top with champagne or prosecco. Garnish with fresh orange peels on the rim before serving.

Summer

CLASSIC NEW ENGLAND CLAMBAKE MENU

Classic New England Clambake
Lobster, Clams, Mussels, Corn, Potatoes, and Kielbasa

Prosciutto, Cantaloupe, and Mint Salad

Heirloom Tomato Salad
Served with Gorgonzola Dressing Dip

Gorgonzola Dressing Dip

Fresh Basil Pesto and Rigatoni

Chive Potato Salad

Warm Buttered Lobster Rolls
Made with Leftover Lobster Meat

I'VE STARTED AN ANNUAL TRADITION OF WRIT-ING A SUMMER BUCKET LIST. It's like a New Year's resolution guide for the summer months, except instead of things like eating healthier and working out, I fill it with fun ideas for special summer-only activities. Summer can be fleeting in New England; we get two full warm months if we're lucky. I make it my mission to pack our schedule from the 4th of July to Labor Day with things like beach days, picnics, bonfires, and road trips up and down the coast. This past summer my husband and I added one particular item to our summer bucket list that I was so excited to mark off: *hosting a clambake*.

I love reading about the grittiness and history of a traditional clambake, with the grueling work of digging a large pit, collecting seaweed, and keeping a fire rolling. Truthfully though, this large-scale cooking method was a bit intimidating for me to attempt. Our version takes inspiration from the history, tradition, and ingredients of a true New England clambake. Where it differs is in the execution; we layered our clambake elements in a large lobster pot that heats on a propane-fueled heating element and steams all the ingredients in much less time.

Going into my first clambake-hosting experience, I realized there were a few misconceptions about the meal. The first is that a clambake is a very expensive dinner to host. At the height of lobster season, prices come down quite a bit locally, and we planned the gathering around this time period. The other ingredients like clams and mussels, potatoes, and corn are also affordable when purchased at the height of the summer season. Waiting for these elements of the dish to come in season has the added benefit of being able to source them locally. I love walking to our

neighborhood fish market and seeing the names written on the market's chalkboard listing the local fishing vessels that brought in the shellfish that morning. With several side dishes served alongside the seafood, half a dozen lobsters could feed upward of eight or nine people when shared with the rest of the clambake components.

The other misconception was that the clambake cooking process is a daunting one; it turns out that it's actually quite a simple process. We tested the recipe and methods on a smaller scale a few times before hosting our "official" summer bucket list clambake, and I quickly realized that it was much easier and quicker than expected when using the right tools and doing a bit of prep work. Having a cooking teammate (my husband!) helped a lot when it came to loading the ingredients into the pot layer by layer. Timing each layer is the key to success. Having all of your ingredients prepped and watching the clock for each component's cooking time is all you need to do to execute the clambake smoothly.

When we hosted the clambake with our family, it became a collective cooking experience. Everyone wanted to watch and get involved. We gathered around the pot, with potholders on one hand and cold beers in the other, adding in the next layer of ingredients to steam and infuse with rich seafood flavor. The final unveiling as we pulled the steamer basket out of the water was the grand finale of the cooking process. We unpacked those steamy layers into serving bowls to see what would be enjoyed at our summer feast.

As we sat around enjoying the spoils of our communal cooking, we relished in the results of the clambake. Cooking everything in steam ensures a perfectly done lobster, avoiding the excess water and overcooking that often happens when you boil them submerged in water. The corn on the cob also benefits from the steaming process, with juicy bites full of that brined saltwater flavor blending with the sweetness of the kernels. I love the rich flavor of the kielbasa cooking in the pot and plucked out several pieces from the bowl before we even set it down on the table. Perhaps the best part of the meal, we agreed, was the resulting broth from the pot that we poured over mussels in a big bowl. My father-in-law was the mussel-eating champion at the clam bake, vowing not to let a drop of it go to waste!

The clambake in itself can be a full, self-contained meal. On this particular occasion though, I added tons of extra side dishes to the menu to extend the clambake to a larger crowd. Most of these recipes can be mixed and matched at other barbecues or summer parties. Many of them I make as side dishes for casual weeknight dinners too, like my homemade pesto and the tomato salad with Gorgonzola dressing.

A clambake is a meal meant for sharing, so when it comes to presenting it to guests, I believe that keeping things casual is key. I use raw chambray fabric yardage from a fabric store instead of a tablecloth; it's inexpensive and I won't stress over drips of buttery seafood staining it. Tough enamelware serving pieces are my favorite for outdoor entertaining. A set of simple glass tumblers makes for a great glassware choice for pouring a crisp rosé wine to pair with the meal. Once the table is set and the clambake is ready to serve, all you need to do is crack a lobster, pass a claw, clink cans of cold beer, and let the butter and corn juice drip down your arm. I love the casual gatherings that a meal like this creates, and will be adding it to my annual summer bucket list for years to come.

What's in a Clambake?

You will find many variations in both ingredients and technique for a New England clambake, but most recipes will include four main components that are added to the lobster pot in layers:

Seasoning Elements. The clambake pulls much of its flavor from the briny water that steams up through the shellfish in the pot, but adding other seasoning elements helps infuse flavor back into each ingredient layered in this recipe. Sea salt, whole peppercorns, bay leaves, lemons, celery, onions, and garlic all get wrapped up in a cheesecloth pouch and dunked in the water to create a flavorful broth base. White wine and kielbasa are also added to flavor the broth.

Potatoes. Waxy red potatoes, dropped in the steaming basket whole, are the base layer in the clambake because they take the longest to cook. They taste delicious dunked in the resulting clambake broth and warm melted butter.

Corn. On top of the potato layer, sweet summer corn on the cob gets added to the pot. Break the cobs in half to get more to fit in the pot and create smaller portions for guests' plates. The corn steams in the flavorful broth and is one of my favorite spoils of the clambake layers.

Shellfish. A typical clambake features a variety of shellfish; this version layers small lobsters (chicken, or "chix" size, are a little over a pound each), steamer clams, and mussels. Shell-on shrimp are another common shellfish addition to the pot.

THE CLAMBAKE GEAR

Lobster Pot and Steamer Basket. Every element of the clambake is cooked together in layers, so a large pot is needed to contain the whole meal. We use a thirty-quart stainless steel lobster pot with a fitted steamer basket insert. The steamer basket is helpful to remove all the elements from the pot for serving, while preserving the flavorful broth that results from cooking the seafood and seasoning together in steam.

Heating Element. Given the scale of the lobster pot, we heat ours outdoors on a propane tripod heating element. You can purchase this outdoor propane cooker setup online; it is commonly also used as a turkey fryer during the holidays. Check to see that you have a full propane tank before starting the clambake, to ensure you have enough heat to make it through the cooking process!

Cheesecloth. One of the best results of this seafood-steaming cooking method is the delicious broth that forms in the pot at the end of the cooking time. Cheesecloth allows you to add several ingredients to season the meal and makes removing them from the pot once the cooking is over a simple task. I use the cheesecloth to drop in loosely wrapped packages of clams and mussels into the pot, too. It protects the delicate shells and makes plating the clambake a breeze when you can pluck out the shellfish pouches.

Large Tongs. The scale of the lobster pot and process of continually adding ingredients throughout the cooking process calls for a sturdy set of large tongs. A long set of grilling tongs works well for this recipe.

Sea Salt and Black Peppercorns. A generous amount of sea salt and whole peppercorns are used to create a briny-flavored broth and add flavor to the potatoes and corn. I love to use cleaned oyster shells filled with extra sea salt flakes and freshly cracked black pepper on the table for guests to give a final seasoning to their dish, and bring in a coastal element to your clambake tablescape.

Lobster Tools. To properly dig into the cooked lobster, you'll want to have a set of lobster tools on hand for your guests. A pair of hinged lobster crackers is used for breaking into the claw shells, and lobster picks are used to extract the meat from inside smaller shell crevices. A pair of kitchen shears is also helpful to have on hand for snipping off the rubber bands from lobster claws and cutting open your cheesecloth pouches, and can be used for breaking into some areas of the lobster shells too. Fun additions to the table are seafood shanty–style lobster bibs for your guests; this is a meal where you're expected to get messy!

Shell Bucket. I like to place a large bowl or pail on the edge of the table for guests to drop excess shells in from shucking lobster and cracking into their clams and mussels. It keeps plates clear for digging into many of the clambake elements and side dishes, and makes cleaning up after the dinner a bit easier on the hostess, too. Make sure to keep an eye on the shell bowl or bucket during the meal and empty it out as it gets full!

Warm Butter Bowls. I believe the best part of cracking into a fresh lobster claw is the moment when you get to dunk it into that warm, rich melted butter. A case of four-ounce jelly canning jars is a smart solution for serving individual portions of the warmed butter. You can typically purchase the canning jars at the supermarket. Let them sit in the oven at about 200 degrees, filled with butter, on a rimmed baking sheet to keep the contents warm and melted while you prep the rest of the meal.

Paper Towels. Butter will be dribbling down arms, steamy shellfish will be dripping on the table, and things will get messy! One of the best parts of a clambake is the casual, family-style feasting that takes place once everything is plated on the table. Put a few rolls of paper towels at the ends of your table to keep the mess at bay.

Classic New England Clambake

Lobster, Clams, Mussels, Corn, Potatoes, and Kielbasa

SERVES 6-8

INGREDIENTS

1 yellow onion

1 lemon, plus more for serving

1 head garlic

1 bay leaf

4 celery sticks

2 tablespoons whole black peppercorns

¼ cup sea salt

2 pounds mussels

1 pound steamer clams

3 pounds red potatoes

1 pound sliced kielbasa

6 ears of corn on the cob, halved

2 cups white wine

6-8 lobsters (about 1-1¼ pounds each)

Minced parsley, for garnish

Melted butter, for serving

Salt and black pepper

INSTRUCTIONS

Set up your propane-heated burner outside and bring about 4 inches of water to a boil in a thirty-quart lobster pot. (*Note:* If you don't have this equipment, cut the recipe in half to accommodate to a smaller scale 16-quart stockpot that can be heated on your stovetop.)

Prepare a seasoning pouch by laying out a large square of cheesecloth and placing in the center one peeled and halved onion, one halved lemon, a head of garlic with the top sliced off, a bay leaf, celery, peppercorns, and sea salt.

Tie the opposite corners of the cheesecloth together to create a secure pouch for the seasoning mixture, and drop the pouch in the boiling water.

While the water is being infused with the seasoning pouch, prepare and clean the mussels and clams. Create two more cheesecloth pouches and place the mussels in one and the clams in the other. Tie the opposite corners of the cheesecloth together (loosely this time) to create two pouches.

Insert the steamer basket into the pot and add the potatoes, which should just be covered with water.

Poke the potatoes after 10 minutes with a fork to test their doneness. Once the potatoes are about halfway cooked (just soft to the touch of the fork), add the sliced kielbasa pieces, halved ears of corn, and white wine to the broth mixture. Cook for 5–7 additional minutes.

Open the pot and add the lobsters, then return the lid to the pot and continue to boil for about 7 minutes.

Add the clam and mussel pouches to the top of the pot and boil for another 5 minutes, until the shells open.

Remove the steamer basket from the lobster pot and shake out the remaining broth and liquids before transferring the contents of the basket to serving bowls. I like to divide the clambake into one large bowl for the lobsters, one for potatoes, corn, kielbasa, and clams, and one smaller bowl for the delicate mussels. You can discard the seasoning pouch at the bottom of the pot, but reserve the broth to ladle over the mussels in their serving dish.

Garnish with fresh parsley and serve immediately with melted butter, lemon wedges, salt and pepper, and the rest of your clambake sides.

Tip

Preserve as much of the broth as you can; it has incredible flavor from the seasoning and steam running through the shellfish and kielbasa. Consider using it at a later date as the base for seafood soup or mixed into a shellfish-topped risotto.

Prosciutto, Cantaloupe, and Mint Salad

SERVES 6-8

This simple salad is a warm-weather favorite. The sweet, juicy cantaloupe pieces complement the salty, rich slices of torn prosciutto. I like to dress the salad with ribbons of cool fresh mint, the crisp bite of freshly cracked black pepper, and a drizzle of local honey to tie it all together. I find the simplicity of the ingredients in this recipe makes it work well as a summertime side dish for anything from casual cookouts to more refined dinner parties.

INGREDIENTS

1 medium ripe cantaloupe
¼ pound Italian prosciutto, thinly sliced
1 tablespoon fresh mint leaves
1 tablespoon local honey
Freshly cracked black pepper

INSTRUCTIONS

Use a melon baller to scoop out the ripe cantaloupe. Transfer cantaloupe balls to a serving bowl.

Tear prosciutto slices into 1-inch-wide pieces; roll strips into small rosettes and tuck them in between the cantaloupe pieces.

Chiffonade the fresh mint leaves and sprinkle them evenly over the cantaloupe and prosciutto mixture.

Drizzle the salad with honey and season with freshly cracked black pepper before serving.

Tip

To serve a refreshing chilled dessert for al fresco dining, make this recipe without the prosciutto slices and cracked black pepper for a sweeter result. Individually spearing the cantaloupe pieces with ribbons of prosciutto on toothpicks before dressing with honey, mint, and pepper can also elevate this dish for a bite-size appetizer.

Heirloom Tomato Salad
Served with Gorgonzola Dressing Dip

SERVES 6

There are few ingredients at the farmer's market that I'm more drawn to than gorgeous heirloom tomatoes. Each one is an individual work of art, the colors and shapes as unique as fingerprints. I love to use them at the peak of their freshness in a bright and rustic summer salad. The tomatoes are arranged over a bed of crisp lettuce leaves and topped with chopped chives, a generous seasoning of sea salt and black pepper, and dollops of my homemade Gorgonzola Dressing Dip. I slice the large tomatoes into discs, halve and quarter the medium-size ones, and leave some of the smaller tomatoes whole for a variety of textures on the plate.

INGREDIENTS

1 medium head bibb lettuce
1 pound heirloom tomatoes, variety of sizes
1 tablespoon fresh chives, minced
Salt and black pepper
¼ cup crumbled Gorgonzola cheese
Gorgonzola Dressing Dip (see page 65)

INSTRUCTIONS

Wash and dry lettuce, tomatoes, and chives.

On a chilled platter, arrange the lettuce leaves in a single layer.

On top of the lettuce, add the heirloom tomatoes in a variety of sizes; slice larger tomatoes, quarter and halve medium tomatoes, and leave a few smaller tomatoes whole.

Sprinkle minced fresh chives over the top of the tomatoes; season the tomatoes generously with salt and pepper.

Finish the salad with Gorgonzola crumbles and spoon homemade Gorgonzola dressing dip on top immediately before serving.

Gorgonzola Dressing Dip

SERVES 6-8

Is it a dressing? Or is it a dip? I say it can be both! I love to make this thick, creamy salad dressing to serve with the Heirloom Tomato Salad in the summer. The dressing recipe can double as a simple dip as well; I like to serve it with spicy grilled turkey burgers or to dunk buffalo chicken wings in for a cool complement to the hot sauce heat. It's simple to assemble and lasts in the fridge for a day or two after preparing, so consider making it ahead of your salad assembly.

INGREDIENTS

¾ cup sour cream

2 tablespoons mayonnaise

1½ tablespoons red wine vinegar

1 tablespoon minced fresh chives

½ cup Gorgonzola crumbles

Black pepper

INSTRUCTIONS

In a bowl, combine sour cream, mayonnaise, red wine vinegar, minced fresh chives, and Gorgonzola crumbles.

Season with black pepper to taste and refrigerate at least 30 minutes before serving.

Tip

You can easily swap out Gorgonzola for another crumbly blue cheese in this recipe and serve alongside spicy chicken wings with fresh carrot and celery sticks.

Fresh Basil Pesto and Rigatoni

SERVES 6-8

One of the best signs of summer is an abundance of fresh basil leaves pouring out of garden beds. In fact, it's one of the very few plants in my garden that I can manage to keep alive—I lack the green thumb gene! A great way to use basil from your garden (or local farmer's market) is with a simple, fragrant homemade pesto sauce tossed with al dente rigatoni and tons of salty grated Parmesan cheese.

The benefit of pesto is that even loosely following a recipe will yield good results. I've played around with proportions and ingredients and landed on this combination with a hint of citrus bite from the lemon juice and just a touch of garlic flavoring from one clove. Experimentation can yield other tasty variations too; consider adding walnuts or cashews in lieu of pine nuts, or mix in other herbs like mint leaves to evolve the classic pesto flavor. Other pasta shapes also work well; I always look for something with ridges (like a cavatappi or medium shells) to grip all the bright green sauce on each bite.

This recipe yields about three-quarters cup pesto, which is enough to coat one pound of pasta. It easily doubles or triples if you have a bounty of basil to use up, and can keep in the refrigerator for about a week.

INGREDIENTS

1 pound rigatoni

2 cups fresh basil leaves

1 garlic clove

2 tablespoons toasted pine nuts

2 tablespoons fresh lemon juice

⅓ cup extra-virgin olive oil

2 tablespoons grated Parmesan cheese, plus more for garnish

Salt and black pepper

¼ cup reserved pasta water

INSTRUCTIONS

Bring a pot of salted water to a boil and cook rigatoni to al dente, reserving about ¼ cup of the pasta water before draining.

In a blender or food processor, combine fresh basil leaves, garlic, pine nuts, lemon juice, and olive oil; blend to combine.

Stir in grated Parmesan cheese to the pesto and season to taste with salt and pepper.

Toss pesto with drained rigatoni and a spoonful of the reserved pasta water, coating each noodle. Add more pasta water if necessary to loosen the sauce.

Serve warm and garnish with additional Parmesan cheese.

Tip

Have extra pine nuts left over from this recipe? Freeze them in a sealed container to preserve their freshness; they'll keep in the freezer for about nine months. Defrost them with a quick toast in a frying pan over medium heat and add them to other pasta dishes, salads, or a fresh batch of pesto at a later date.

Chive Potato Salad

This potato salad is a family favorite at summer events and is based on a recipe my mother made for barbecues when we were kids. I always start with small red potatoes and keep on the waxy, flavorful skins for both added color and texture. The dressing is made up of equal parts mayonnaise and sour cream and a generous seasoning of salt and pepper for added flavor. A tiny bit of apple cider vinegar goes into the dressing for a subtle tang, and the whole mixture gets tossed with the cooked red potatoes and a large heap of finely chopped chives. The chives have a bright, crisp onion flavor that balances the creaminess of the dressing and potatoes. I find this recipe always tastes better when made ahead and stored in the fridge before serving.

INGREDIENTS

2 pounds small red potatoes

¼ cup sour cream

¼ cup mayonnaise

½ tablespoon apple cider vinegar

¼ cup minced fresh chives

Salt and black pepper

INSTRUCTIONS

Boil a large pot of salted water and prepare potatoes, cutting them into about 1-inch pieces (halve smaller potatoes, quarter larger ones).

Cook potatoes through until they are slightly softened. To test, remove a potato from the water and place it on a cutting board. Use the back of a fork to press down on the potato; it should break under medium pressure from the fork.

Drain the potatoes and let them cool for at least 15 minutes while you prepare the dressing.

To make the dressing, whisk together the sour cream, mayonnaise, and vinegar.

Toss the dressing mixture over the potatoes and then fold in the minced chives.

Season with salt and pepper and refrigerate at least 2 hours before serving.

Tip

This potato salad recipe tastes best when the flavors blend together in the refrigerator before serving. Consider making this the night before your barbecue for the best flavors, making sure to stir the potato salad and garnish with additional fresh chives before serving. The potato salad also makes great leftovers to serve alongside the Warm Buttered Lobster Rolls (see page 69).

Warm Buttered Lobster Rolls

Made with Leftover Lobster Meat

SERVES 2

My version of the classic lobster roll is tossed with just a few ingredients for flavor, along with warm, melted butter. I serve them with the Chive Potato Salad (see page 68), which tastes great as a leftover side dish from the lobster bake, and New England–style crunchy, kettle-cooked potato chips.

INGREDIENTS

3 tablespoons butter, divided

2 rolls or hot dog buns

6 ounces chopped cooked lobster meat (2 lobsters, about 1 pound each)

1 tablespoon fresh lemon juice

⅛ teaspoon Old Bay Seasoning

Black pepper

Bibb lettuce

Fresh chives, minced, for garnish

INSTRUCTIONS

In a saucepan, heat 1 tablespoon butter until melted.

Brush melted butter on the top of two rolls or hot dog buns and place on a baking sheet. Lightly toast the rolls in a 450°F oven for 5 minutes, or until they're golden brown and warmed.

Heat the remaining 2 tablespoons butter in the saucepan over medium heat until fully melted.

Toss the chopped lobster meat pieces in the butter, spooning butter continuously over the top of the meat for 2–3 minutes.

Remove lobster and butter mixture from heat and fold in the fresh lemon juice; season with Old Bay and freshly cracked black pepper.

Line the inside of each toasted bun with bib lettuce leaves and divide the warm, buttered lobster between the two buns.

Top each lobster roll with a drizzle of the remaining butter from the pan and garnish with minced fresh chives before serving.

BERRY PICKING POTLUCK MENU

Berry Crostini
Blueberry, Ricotta, and Lemon Zest
Raspberry, Thyme, Goat Cheese, and Honey

Blackberry Naan Flatbread
With Charred Corn and Fontina Cheese

Strawberry Orzo Salad
With Almond Slices and Parmesan Cheese

Berry Cheesecake Jars
With Blueberry Reduction

Blueberry Cobbler
Grandma Ida's Famous Family Recipe

Berry Herb DIY Cocktail Bar
Blueberry Lemon Simple Syrup
Raspberry Mint Simple Syrup
Strawberry Thyme Simple Syrup

I JUST CAN'T HELP MYSELF WHEN I SEE THE
NEATLY ORGANIZED ROWS OF CARDBOARD
BERRY BASKETS lined up on the table at summer farm stands,
overflowing with blueberries and strawberries, raspberries and blackberries. I reach for my back pocket to grab my phone and start snapping
pictures of the bright, rich colors in an effort to capture the visual feast.
Before I've even taken a bite of their sweet and tart flavors, I am absolutely smitten with the season's bounty of berries.

Berry picking in New England seems to have become as commonplace
as a day at the apple orchard in the fall. It is a picturesque activity with
the added bonus of coming home toting plenty of fresh little sweet fruit
morsels. I personally like to do my berry hunting at farm stands. My husband and I took a weekend road trip to Maine a few years ago; we were on
the hunt for the state's best lobster roll. On the drive though, we found
something almost more delectable than warm buttery lobster: fresh blueberries. We drove a long and winding farm-lined road to find a coveted
lobster roll shack, and along that route were some of the most amazing
berry-filled farm stands. I'm talking about those old-fashioned, honor-
system-run farm stands—a folding table with a beach umbrella tied to it
to shade the berries and some of the most delicious looking produce I've
ever seen.

Inspired by these fruity, juicy little berry bites, I thought that berries
would be the perfect theme for a potluck party. A themed potluck party
is one of my favorite ways to celebrate flavors of the season, experience
new recipes, and gather my friends together for an afternoon of snacks
and sips. I've done this before on a few occasions, each time picking a

different theme. A chips and dip–themed party was my very first themed potluck party, which resulted in a dozen of my buddies bringing wildly different and delicious dips for us to try. In the fall I've hosted an apples and pumpkins–themed party and had guests bring their favorite apple and pumpkin–themed recipes. A berry-themed party felt like the essential way to celebrate these summer ingredients.

So how exactly do you go about hosting a themed potluck party? To start, invite your guests and ask them to pick a recipe. I tell my friends to share their recipe with me in advance so that I can make sure we have a variety of dishes. Next, I plan my own menu based on what others are bringing. If I know I have six friends bringing desserts, I'll fill in the blanks with appetizers and salads. As the hostess I make sure to provide a good range of dishes so that we end up with a well-rounded meal of snacks and sweets. I find that a range of small bites and scoopable salads work best for this type of party, so that attendees can fill their plate with a little taste of everything.

I also make sure to add a signature cocktail to the menu that matches the theme of the event. For this berry-inspired menu I made a series of simple syrups that can be mixed and matched to create custom drinks. It's a fun way to get guests involved in crafting drinks to match their tastes.

Decorating your table for a themed potluck party is simple, because you've already picked a theme! For my chips and dip party, I created a centerpiece with tiered serving dishes that featured several different types of chips and dipping accompaniments. At the apples and pumpkins potluck, I decorated the table with big bowls of red apples and nestled a variety of seasonal pumpkins and gourds around the serving dishes. The very same berry baskets that caught my eye at the farm stand are a perfect vessel for decorating around this theme. I use the inexpensive, recycled cardboard baskets to hold bread and crackers on a cheeseboard or cut vegetables on a crudité platter. Put small jars inside the baskets to contain your silverware or to create small flower arrangements. Fill the baskets with leftover fresh berries to add pops of color to the table and allow guests to snack on the star ingredients.

You can design some fun activities out of partygoers nibbling on a variety of dishes inspired by the berry potluck theme. If you have a competitive crowd, make things interesting with prizes for the best appetizer, salad, and dessert. Let guests vote on the dishes, and have a prize for the "best-in-show" dish at the table. You can also line up berries in bowls from different local farms and have guests do a blind taste test and rate their favorites. Take a note from a wine tasting and give guests cards to score and describe the berries, to reveal the party's favorite varieties.

At the end of the party, I love to send guests home with a little treat to remember the occasion. Wrap up a box of a berry baked treat or a bottle of their own berry-infused simple syrup, and pair it with a stack of cards featuring the recipes that all the guests shared with you before the event. Or send a note a few days after the party thanking everyone for attending and share a digital copy of the most coveted berry potluck recipes.

Berry Crostini

Blueberry, Ricotta, and Lemon Zest
Raspberry, Thyme, Goat Cheese, and Honey

SERVES 8-12

Crostini. It sounds so fancy, doesn't it? It's really just a tiny little toast, but it's a tiny little toast that can do so much. To highlight the delicious berries of the season, add thin-sliced strawberries to it—so delectable and sweet—to the goat cheese toast base. Another spin on this layered berry and cheese crostini concept takes a smooth ricotta cheese and tops it with the tart flavors of blueberries and fresh citrus zest from a lemon. Both crostini recipes are delicious on their own, but I love to serve them side by side to let the colors and flavors play off one another.

INGREDIENTS

1 large baguette
Olive oil

Blueberry, Ricotta, and Lemon Zest

½ cup ricotta cheese
⅓ cup blueberries
1 tablespoon lemon zest

Raspberry, Thyme, Goat Cheese, and Honey

½ cup goat cheese
⅓ cup sliced raspberries
1 tablespoon fresh thyme leaves
1½ tablespoons honey

INSTRUCTIONS

Slice the baguette into 1-inch rounds and transfer to a large baking sheet.

Lightly drizzle the bread with olive oil and place in the oven under the broiler for about 2 minutes total, flipping halfway through to toast both sides. Remove once the bread is a golden brown.

Divide the toasts between two serving plates. Spread a spoonful of ricotta cheese on half of the toasts, and spread a spoonful of goat cheese on the other half of the toasts.

Top the ricotta toasts with three or four blueberries and sprinkle with freshly grated lemon zest. Top the goat cheese toasts with slices of raspberries and fresh thyme leaves, then drizzle with honey.

Blackberry Naan Flatbread

With Charred Corn and Fontina Cheese

SERVES 4

Berries happen to come in season around the same time that delicious summer corn is also becoming available from local farms; both ingredients have their own unique sweetness that tastes like summer. I combined the flavors on an easy-to-assemble flatbread pizza for an appetizer that can be on the table in just a matter of minutes. For the flatbread base, I use store-bought naan. The fluffy texture crisps up just a bit under high heat to hold its structure under the cheese and toppings. A salty fontina cheese balances the sweet flavors of the berries and grilled corn, and melts beautifully and quickly under the high heat. I slice the pieces into small strips for easy snacking during a party, but this flatbread also makes for a great weeknight dinner in the summer too!

INGREDIENTS

1 piece naan
¾ cup shredded fontina cheese
¼ cup fresh blackberries
½ cup grilled corn kernels
Olive oil
Salt and black pepper
Fresh basil leaves

INSTRUCTIONS

Preheat oven to 425°F.

Line a rimmed baking sheet with parchment paper and place the naan on the baking sheet.

Evenly distribute the shredded fontina cheese on the naan, leaving a bit of room around the edges for a crust.

Prepare the blackberries by slicing larger berries in half; prepare the grilled corn by removing the charred kernels from the cob.

Top the naan with blackberries and grilled corn, spreading them evenly on top of the cheese.

Drizzle the top of the flatbread with just a bit of olive oil, and lightly season with salt and pepper.

Bake at 425°F for about 7 minutes, until cheese melts and the edges of the naan toast and crisp.

Remove from oven and top with chopped fresh basil; slice naan into small strips before serving.

Strawberry Orzo Salad
With Almond Slices and Parmesan Cheese
SERVES 6–8

One of my favorite things about cooking with berries is that their sweetness is often a delicious counterpart to the saltiness of sharp cheese flavors, like the nutty Parmesan cheese used in this recipe. When I first tested this recipe, I set it out on the counter at my parents' house and within minutes saw family members swarming around it, dipping spoons in to grab tastes. It turns out that the sweet and savory balance worked, and I had to fight them off to get the last spoonful. This salad will always be in my back pocket for a summer potluck dish now because of the colorful ingredients, crowd-pleasing flavors, and how well it serves at room temperature.

INGREDIENTS

1 pound orzo
1½ cups roughly chopped fresh spinach
¾ cup shredded Parmesan cheese
1½ cups roughly chopped strawberries
½ cup sliced almonds
3 tablespoons balsamic vinegar
Salt and black pepper

INSTRUCTIONS

Cook box of orzo as directed, drain, and transfer to a large serving bowl.

While the orzo is still warm, stir in the spinach and Parmesan cheese. The spinach will wilt and the cheese will melt into the orzo.

Set the orzo aside to cool for about 10 minutes, then fold in the chopped strawberries and sliced almonds.

Drizzle the salad with balsamic vinegar; stir to fully combine the ingredients and coat with the vinegar.

Season with salt and pepper to taste before serving.

Berry Cheesecake Jars

With Blueberry Reduction

SERVES 8

Entertaining in the warmth of summer can have its challenges, but this dessert recipe keeps my kitchen cool and my friends refreshed.

It all starts with a simple shortcut: a store-bought frozen cheesecake. I chop up that frozen cheesecake and layer the cold cubes and crumbly graham cracker crust bits into small mason jars, and then top them with a sweet and sticky blueberry reduction. Each jar gets finished with any fresh berries that I have on hand—a mixture of reds and blues that are perfect for a patriotic summer celebration. A garnish of fresh mint adds just a bit more coolness to this half-frozen dessert, which is absolutely refreshing to bite into on a hot summer day.

INGREDIENTS

For Blueberry Reduction

½ cup granulated sugar

2 cups blueberries

1 tablespoon lemon juice

For Cheesecake Jars

1 frozen New York–style cheesecake

2 cups mixed fresh berries of your choice

Blueberry reduction

Fresh mint leaves, for garnish

INSTRUCTIONS

To make the blueberry reduction, combine sugar, blueberries, and lemon juice in a small saucepan and simmer for 20 minutes, until the berries begin to break down and the sauce thickens.

Remove reduction from stove and strain the mixture through a mesh strainer, pressing down on the berries to release all the juices.

Discard the berries and let the remaining liquid cool in a bowl until ready to use.

To assemble the jars, cut the frozen cheesecake into eight slices and then cut each slice into small cubes. Evenly distribute the frozen cheesecake cubes into eight small mason jars.

Divide the blueberry reduction among the jars, pouring the sauce over the frozen cheesecake.

Top each jar with about ¼ cup fresh berries and finish with sprigs of fresh mint.

Tip

If you don't plan to serve these cheesecake jars immediately, screw the tops on the mason jars and keep them chilled until ready to serve; they hold up well in a cooler on ice. Remove them from the freezer or cooler fifteen minutes before serving, and the cheesecake will thaw just enough to be a cold, refreshing treat.

Blueberry Cobbler

Grandma Ida's Famous Family Recipe

SERVES 6

We have a few summer traditions that are absolute essentials for our family, and one is particularly tasty: making Grandma's homemade blueberry cobbler recipe. I can almost assemble it blindfolded, we've made it so many times, but I love pulling out the flour- and butter-stained index card that my grandmother wrote the recipe on years ago. The pencil marks that firmly scrolled out "Do not stir!"—a key instruction in the recipe—are fading, but my memories of making this with her as a kid never will. To me, each bite tastes like a burst of summer. The warm blueberries scooped out onto a plate with melting vanilla bean ice cream served over the top are absolute bliss.

INGREDIENTS

½ cup (1 stick) butter

1 cup flour

1 teaspoon baking powder

1½ cups granulated sugar, divided

½ cup milk

2 cups blueberries

1 tablespoon fresh lemon juice

Vanilla ice cream, for serving

INSTRUCTIONS

Preheat oven to 350°F and melt butter in a deep round casserole dish while the oven is heating up.

In a bowl, sift together flour and baking powder; combine with 1 cup of the sugar and milk. Stir until the ingredients are incorporated and set batter aside.

In a small saucepan, combine remaining ½ cup sugar, blueberries, and lemon juice; simmer for 7–10 minutes.

Pour batter over the melted butter in the warm casserole dish, and then pour the blueberry mixture over the batter (*but do not stir!*).

Bake at 350°F for 45 minutes, until golden brown.

Serve warm with vanilla ice cream.

Tip

Family secret: it's totally fine to use frozen blueberries in this recipe. Just make sure to strain a tiny bit of the excess liquid out of the blueberry mixture in your saucepan. Frozen blueberries tend to release more liquid than fresh berries when heated. Don't throw that liquid away though! You can further reduce it and use it as a syrup in cocktails or drizzle it on some vanilla ice cream.

Berry Herb DIY Cocktail Bar

Blueberry Lemon Simple Syrup
Raspberry Mint Simple Syrup
Strawberry Thyme Simple Syrup

SERVES 8-12 EACH

An interactive bar is a great party trick. Giving your party attendees a few options to build their own cocktail is a fun way to get them involved, and frees up the hostess to tend to other details while they're DIY-ing their drinks! Your guests can pick their syrup flavors or mix and match a combination of them, add them into a cocktail base of their choice, and garnish their drink with a variety of berries, citrus, and herbs. It's also a great option for non-alcoholic drinks with unflavored soda water.

INGREDIENTS

For Blueberry Lemon Simple Syrup

½ cup blueberries
¼ cup fresh lemon juice
1 tablespoon lemon zest
½ cup granulated sugar
½ cup water

For Raspberry Mint Simple Syrup

¾ cup raspberries
½ cup fresh mint leaves
½ cup granulated sugar
½ cup water

For Strawberry Thyme Simple Syrup

¾ cup strawberries, stems removed
6-8 fresh thyme sprigs
½ cup granulated sugar
½ cup water

INSTRUCTIONS

For each simple syrup, combine ingredients in a small saucepan and simmer for about 20 minutes, until reduced by half.

Remove from stove and strain remaining herbs and berries out of the liquid.

Use a small funnel to transfer the syrups into glass containers and chill until ready to use.

Pour syrups over chilled sparkling wine or unflavored soda water to make berry-flavored cocktails. Garnish with additional berries and herbs.

Tip

Get creative with presentation! Collect a variety of glass bottles and purchase pouring spouts to fit into the bottles to make the syrups easy to dispense. Label the bottles with decorative tags and add a handwritten menu on a chalkboard with instructions for guests to build their own custom cocktail with the syrups, berries, herbs, and sparkling wine or soda water.

GRILLED PIZZA
DINNER PARTY MENU

Homemade Pizza Dough

Pizza Crust Seasoning

Simple Pizza Sauce

Marinated Olives

Roasted Garlic

Roasted Tomatoes

Roasted Tomato Pizza Knots

Pizza Antipasto Salad
With Roasted Garlic Balsamic Vinaigrette

Grilled Sausage and Marinated Olive Pizza

Grilled Summer Vegetable Pizza

Grilled Goat Cheese and Tomato Pizza

PIZZA HOLDS A SPECIAL PLACE IN MY HEART.

For as long as I can remember, Friday night at my house has been pizza night. Growing up, we'd get a large pizza that was half cheese, half some other topping that was greatly debated in the hours leading up to 6 p.m. The tradition lives on into adulthood in our charming little coastal town; we pick up a few take-out pizzas and meet our friends for Friday night "beach pizza" at the nearby town beach. Everyone passes around the cardboard boxes and paper plates and picks out their favorite slices to enjoy with the cold beverages we brought to share. There's a reason that it's such a great Friday night meal: It's casual, it's comforting, and it's meant to be shared.

Pizza isn't just a takeout option though; it's a delicious meal to make at home, too. When my husband and I got married, we registered for all sorts of kitchen gadgets and cooking tools and beautiful serving pieces. A pizza stone was one of those items on the list, and I remember some-one scoffed, "Oh, you'll use that once and then it will gather dust in your cabinet." Turns out they were quite wrong; we heat up that pizza stone on our grill all summer long and churn out crispy, bubbly, hot homemade pizzas. One of the reasons we use it so often is because we figured out how to make a pizza at home that matches our expectations of delicious pizzeria pizza.

The Tools. The reason that a pizza from a pizzeria often tastes so very different from a homemade pizza is the tools that they are using. The most important of those tools is the pizza oven. I would love to have a big wood-fired pizza oven in our backyard, but there are lots more press-ing home projects that have to take place before that dream comes true.

In the meantime a good pizza stone and a grill make for a great makeshift pizza oven. Your grill can likely get much hotter than the oven in your kitchen—and heat is exactly what makes pizza cook quickly, for a crispy yet fluffy crust. The pizza stone also helps mimic the effects of a pizza oven; the porous nature of the surface absorbs moisture, which also helps crisp the dough into a tasty crust.

The Ingredients. This seems pretty obvious, but ingredients matter. This is true of *any* recipe, but seems especially true of pizza. Homemade pizza dough, a quality tomato sauce, and fresh mozzarella are the difference between a good pizza and a great pizza.

The Toppings. Get creative! And use what you have available. Some of my best pizza creations have come from pulling leftover ingredients from the refrigerator and pantry for inspiration. A chopped-up breaded chicken cutlet, a ladle of leftover Bolognese sauce, a dash of seasonal herbs from the garden, or fresh produce from the farmer's market have all been ingredients that resulted in show-stopping pizzas at our house.

The Party. *Everyone loves pizza.* Hosting friends for a make-your-own pizza night is one of the best ways to entertain. Prepare the dough, sauce, and toppings and set it all out to let everyone create pizzas that fit their tastes. They're quick on and off the grill, and it makes for a fun, interactive experience where everyone gets a slice of their favorite flavors.

THE SECRETS TO PIZZA DOUGH SUCCESS

Flour. Given that the number of ingredients in pizza dough is so stream-lined, the quality and type of those ingredients can matter a lot. I tested a few different types of flour in my dough experiments and found that a mixture of all-purpose flour with "00" (finely milled) flour yielded the best results.

Water. The temperature of the water used in the dough recipe has a nar-row window of range to produce a good result. Too cold and the yeast won't become active, too hot and you could kill the yeast; 105–110°F is the ideal water temperature.

Mixing. I tried the dough hook on my stand mixer and a food processor for mixing together the ingredients, but I find the best results come from pulling the dough together with my hands until just combined to avoid overworking it.

Stretching. Use your hands to stretch the dough, working from the center and slightly pulling the edges while gravity works to pull the dough into a large shape. Stretch the dough to about a 14-inch circle, let it rest for a minute or two and retract, and then press out the edges a bit more while it's on your work surface to get a consistent thickness and shape.

Transferring. Your pizza stone should be heating up on the grill as you prepare your pizza, which means that at some point, you have to transfer the sticky pizza dough covered in sauce and cheese and toppings from your work surface to the pizza stone. I add just a tiny dusting of cornmeal to a rimless baking sheet to prevent sticking, then run a large flat spatula under the dough to loosen any sticking areas before sliding it onto the stone. It doesn't always turn out perfectly, so if your toppings get jostled in the transfer, quickly push them back into place with a grill spatula or long tongs before closing the grill to cook.

Heat. Letting the grill and pizza stone both preheat for a fair amount of time makes a big impact. Turn the grill on before you start preparing the meal and let the stone heat up for at least 20 minutes to ensure the pizza will cook and crisp quickly.

Homemade Pizza Dough

SERVES 8

Of all the recipes that I tested for this book, this pizza dough was my biggest undertaking. Pizza dough is so simple—most recipes call for just four or five ingredients—and yet tiny alterations within those ingredients can produce vastly different results. After all my tests (and lots of pizza taste-testing, a very serious job) and research (I read five different books on pizza and dozens of articles on pizza dough techniques), I now rely on this simple recipe.

INGREDIENTS

¼ teaspoon active dry yeast

1½ cups warm water (about 110°F)

3¼ cups flour (ideally an even blend of all-purpose flour and 00 flour)

2½ teaspoons salt

1 teaspoon granulated sugar

Extra flour and cornmeal for dusting your work surface

INSTRUCTIONS

Add the yeast to a bowl and pour the warm water over the yeast to activate it; let sit for 5 minutes.

In a separate bowl, measure and sift together the flour, salt, and sugar.

Add the dry ingredients to the yeast bowl and mix with your hands until a shaggy dough forms.

Divide the dough into two equal portions and roll them into balls, place each dough ball in a bowl, and cover tightly with plastic wrap.

Let the dough rise for at least 12 hours, and up to 24 hours for ideal results.

When ready to use, remove the plastic wrap and punch the risen dough down into the bowl.

Remove from bowl and lightly knead the dough to revert to a ball shape, then begin to stretch it into your desired crust shape. Dough should provide enough for two 14-inch-round pizzas.

Pizza Crust Seasoning

SERVES 8

When you make the same recipes on a regular basis, you often don't think of them as recipes at all. It becomes second nature to add a dash of this and a pinch of that, and that's certainly the case with this pizza crust seasoning. During pizza-making sessions at our house, we're usually gathered around our kitchen island with a few cold beers in hand and flour dusting the butcher-block countertop. I go through the motions of seasoning the crust with this combination of spices that live on the ledge above my stove without even thinking (we use them so often that they have been elevated from the spice cabinet to "ledge status").

Adding just a touch of seasoning to the crust gives it beautiful texture when it comes off the grill, and lots of flavor too. In our house we always serve our pizza with a collection of hot sauces, and dipping the seasoned crust in a dash of hot sauce is one of my favorite bites of the whole meal.

INGREDIENTS

½ teaspoon sea salt

½ teaspoon red pepper flakes

½ teaspoon dried oregano

½ teaspoon garlic powder

½ teaspoon onion powder

INSTRUCTIONS

In a bowl, combine all spices and mix together until fully incorporated.

Use the mixture to season the crust of your pizza before you assemble and grill it.

Simple Pizza Sauce

SERVES 8

Can you use a jar of store-bought tomato sauce on your pizza? Sure you can. I'll tell you a little secret: I do it too; in a pinch it works just fine. If you're going through the effort to prepare a delicious homemade dough though, why not whip together a quick homemade tomato sauce that is going to taste amazing and bring your pizza to the next level?

This sauce uses crushed, canned tomatoes for the base. If you can, try to find San Marzano canned tomatoes, which are known for their sweet flavor and low acidity. The sauce is lightly seasoned with sautéed garlic, red pepper flakes and oregano, and just a dash of sugar for the sweetness that is common in a pizza sauce. Another important ingredient is the butter, which also adds a smoothness to the sauce that you wouldn't get with olive oil.

We love our weekly Friday pizza nights when it's warm enough to be grilling, so if I'm making a batch of this sauce I sometimes double it and store it in the fridge to last me two occasions. It should keep for up to two weeks in a well-sealed glass jar.

INGREDIENTS

3 tablespoons butter

3 cloves garlic, minced

1 teaspoon dried oregano

1 teaspoon red pepper flakes

2 cups crushed tomatoes

1 teaspoon granulated sugar

1 teaspoon salt

1 teaspoon black pepper

¼ cup grated Parmesan cheese

INSTRUCTIONS

In a saucepan, heat butter over medium heat and add finely minced garlic to the pan.

Sauté the garlic until softened and golden in color; stir in the oregano and red pepper flakes and cook for an additional 1–2 minutes.

Add crushed tomatoes, sugar, salt, and pepper and simmer for about 30 minutes.

Remove from stove and stir in Parmesan cheese to finish.

Tip

Upgrade the sauce for different recipes by making a few simple ingredient additions. For a bright, fresh summery sauce, I like to add freshly minced basil leaves; for a heartier sauce for cool fall nights, I'll add some browned ground beef and ¼ cup red wine.

Marinated Olives

SERVES 8

Specialty grocery store olive bars are beautifully enticing to browse, but those gourmet olives tend to be rather expensive. Making your own marinated olives at home is as easy as can be, saves a pretty penny, and gives you lots of control over the exact flavors you want in your recipe. This version has a balance of herbs and citrus with just a touch of heat from the red pepper and garlic.

There are tons of uses for marinated olives when entertaining besides slicing them up on your pizza. I use them in my Pizza Antipasto Salad (see page 97) that I serve with the pizza, and they make a shining addition to a cheeseboard or mezze platter as an appetizer for guests. The flavor of the marinade develops over a few days, so feel free to make them in advance of your pizza party, if you can resist eating them all before then!

INGREDIENTS

½ cup olive oil

1 teaspoon lemon zest

1 teaspoon orange zest

1 teaspoon red pepper flakes

1 clove garlic, minced

3 sprigs fresh rosemary

3 sprigs fresh thyme

1 bay leaf

2 cups mixed olives

INSTRUCTIONS

Combine olive oil with citrus zest, red pepper flakes, finely minced garlic, and herbs in a saucepan and heat to combine for about 15 minutes.

Remove the pan from the stove and let mixture cool before tossing the mixed olives with the infused olive oil mixture.

Transfer the olives with the herbs and oil into a lidded jar. Refrigerate for at least 24 hours to let the flavors marinate the olives.

Remove the olives from the refrigerator 1 hour before serving; discard bay leaf and herb stems.

Roasted Garlic

SERVES 4-6

Long before my husband and I were dating, we went on our first date but didn't realize it. Still in the friend zone, my adorable husband schemed up a plan where I would help him write an English paper in exchange for a dinner out at a nice Italian restaurant.

The Boston chain restaurant felt pretty darn fancy to a teenage college student, with their white tablecloths and big red leather booths. Before our entrees were served, the restaurant placed big bowls of fluffy focaccia bread on the table with a bowl of olive oil for dipping and a whole head of roasted garlic. It was so delicious, and since I was certain this wasn't a date, I ate that whole bowl of roasted garlic with abandon.

I am happy to report that we eventually fell in love, had dinner dates that I knew were actually dates, got married, had a baby, and still eat garlic like it's going out of style. The restaurant that served that delicious roasted garlic closed down, but it's easy to re-create it at home with this simple recipe that you can use in dozens of ways. Fold it into butter to make a roasted garlic spread, blend it into roasted garlic hummus, whisk it into salad dressings, add into pasta dishes, and use it on your pizza too.

INGREDIENTS

1 large head garlic
Olive oil
Sea salt

INSTRUCTIONS

Preheat oven to 400°F.

Peel away any loose layers on the outside of the garlic head. Using a sharp knife, slice off about ¼ inch of the top of the garlic head, leaving the tops of the cloves exposed.

Place the head of garlic with the exposed cloves facing up on a piece of aluminum foil and drizzle the cloves with a few tablespoons of olive oil.

Sprinkle the exposed cloves with sea salt and wrap the edges of the foil up around the head of garlic to create a sealed packet.

Place the foil-wrapped garlic on a baking sheet and roast at 400°F for 50–60 minutes, until the garlic cloves are softened and golden brown.

Remove the foil from the garlic head and use a small fork to pull the softened cloves out of their skin.

Roasted Tomatoes

SERVES 4-6

Tomatoes are a big part of the essential pizza building blocks. It's not just the tomato sauce, though, where delicious tomatoes can come into play. Roasting whole tomatoes is a great way to bring that sweet summery flavor to a pizza (or many other delicious dishes). The heat caramelizes the sugars in the tomatoes and little bits of charred flavor develop on the tomato skins. You can toss them onto a classic cheese pizza on top of the sauce and mozzarella, or use them in lieu of a red sauce with their flavor and oils replacing a marinara. I also use them in salads and pasta dishes all summer long; in the fall they make a robust addition to a hearty soup. Perhaps the best result of this recipe is the oil that remains in the pan after roasting. The sweet liquids from the tomatoes and seasonings blend into the olive oil; reserve the oil and use it as a dipping sauce, or mix it into a salad dressing for tons of added taste to the dishes you're serving with the pizza.

INGREDIENTS

3 cups cherry and/or grape tomatoes
¼ cup olive oil
½ teaspoon red pepper flakes
½ teaspoon dried oregano
½ teaspoon sea salt
½ teaspoon black pepper

INSTRUCTIONS

Preheat oven to 450°F.

In a baking dish, combine tomatoes with olive oil, herbs, and salt and pepper.

Roast at 450°F for 50–60 minutes; remove from oven when the tomatoes have burst and begin to char.

Remove from baking dish and strain the excess oil and liquid; reserve liquid for other recipes.

Tip

In the summer when there is a bounty of delicious tomatoes, I like to use the roasted garlic recipe and roasted tomato recipe, and combine both ingredients while they're still piping hot over thin spaghetti. As the blistered tomatoes and soft roasted garlic cloves blend with the pasta, they begin to melt into a sauce that delicately coats each piece. A little bit of salt and pepper, freshly chopped basil, and spoonfuls of Parmesan cheese are tossed in to finish this simple dish.

Roasted Tomato Pizza Knots

SERVES 6-8

Garlic knots are the epitome of pizza flavors rolled up into tiny bite-size pieces. The ingredients are simple, but the wow factor in their flavor comes from quickly cooking them directly on the grill grates as you're cooking your pizza.

They are a treat on their own, bursting with flavor from the singed grill lines on the dough. You can also serve them dipped in some olive oil or spread with bits of soft roasted garlic. I like to add a few to my Pizza Antipasto Salad (see page 97) for the full pizza-in-a-bowl experience and, of course, to mop up some of the extra dressing on the plate.

INGREDIENTS
Homemade Pizza Dough (see page 89)

Reserved olive oil from Roasted Tomatoes (see page 95)

Fresh parsley, chopped

INSTRUCTIONS
Preheat grill to 500°F.

Roll and cut pizza dough into approximately 4- x 1-inch pieces.

Tie the dough pieces to form knot shapes; lightly roll the dough in the reserved roasted tomato olive oil.

Place the knotted dough directly onto the grates of the grill and cook for about 3 minutes before rotating.

Cook on the remaining side for another 3 minutes, until the knot turns a golden brown with dark grill marks on the dough.

Remove from grill and sprinkle with chopped fresh parsley.

Serve with additional olive oil for dipping, add them to a salad, or spread roasted garlic cloves directly onto the grilled pizza knots.

Tip

To make this recipe quickly without the preparations of homemade pizza dough and the roasted tomato olive oil, substitute fresh store-bought pizza dough and plain olive oil mixed with some minced garlic.

Pizza Antipasto Salad
With Roasted Garlic Balsamic Vinaigrette
SERVES 6-7

A salad is a complement to pizza in every way: from bright and fresh to hearty and savory, cool and crisp to warm and doughy. One weekend I peeked in the fridge to assemble a quick lunch for my family and scanned the shelves to see many leftover ingredients from our Friday night pizza tradition. A few pieces of pepperoni, a jar of olives, leftover slices of provolone cheese, and a bit of that pizza dough from the previous night's batch. Some of my best food ideas come from getting creative with leftovers, and from this selection of ingredients my favorite antipasto salad recipe was born. It's hearty enough to eat on its own as a meal, but it pairs wonderfully with hot, cheesy pizza slices too.

INGREDIENTS

Roasted Garlic Balsamic Vinaigrette
5 Roasted Garlic cloves (see page 93)
¼ cup balsamic vinegar
¼ cup olive oil
1 tablespoon honey
1 teaspoon Dijon mustard
Salt and black pepper

Mixed greens
Sharp provolone cheese
Pepperoni
Fresh parsley
Marinated olives
Parmesan cheese
Red pepper flakes
Roasted Tomato Pizza Knots (see page 96)

INSTRUCTIONS

For the dressing, mash the garlic cloves with the back of a fork and add them to a small mason jar.

Combine balsamic vinegar, olive oil, honey, and Dijon mustard in the jar and season with salt and pepper.

Vigorously shake the jar until the oil and vinegar are fully blended.

Wash and dry mixed greens and place them in a large serving bowl.

Cut pieces of provolone cheese into small cubes, slice pepperoni into thin strips, and mince a small amount of fresh parsley; add to the bowl of mixed greens.

Top the salad with marinated olives and sprinkle with Parmesan cheese and red pepper flakes.

Serve with Roasted Tomato Pizza Knots.

Grilled Sausage and Marinated Olive Pizza

1 PIZZA, SERVES ABOUT 4

My favorite pizza toppings are sausage and olives, and when I think about a classic bite of pizza, those two ingredients are essential. It's a perfect blend of flavors, in my opinion, when spicy sausage crumbles pair with the salty brine of marinated olives and the sweetness of tomato sauce. This pizza is my classic recipe, but I also like to add a few other flavors to it on occasion: roasted garlic cloves spread on the crust underneath the layers of toppings, thin-sliced onions that crisp and caramelize under the heat of the grill, and mushrooms that add an earthiness to each pizza bite. The best part of making your own pizza is that you can choose your own adventure; each slice can have a combination of toppings that is handpicked and carefully placed by you, the pizza maker!

INGREDIENTS

1–2 hot Italian sausage links
¼ cup marinated olives
Homemade Pizza Dough (see page 89)
Cornmeal
Pizza Crust Seasoning (see page 90)
Roasted Garlic cloves (see page 93)
Simple Pizza Sauce (see page 91)
Fresh mozzarella

INSTRUCTIONS

Cook the sausage links on the grill as it begins to preheat to 500°F. Place the pizza stone on the grill to heat up for 20 minutes.

Prepare the olives by removing pits and roughly chopping into small pieces.

On a baking sheet, lightly dust a layer of cornmeal to prevent the dough from sticking. Stretch the dough into a 12- to 14-inch circle.

Season the pizza dough with your pizza crust seasoning spices.

Use the back of a fork to mash a few roasted garlic cloves into the dough; use as many or as few cloves as you like, depending on your taste.

Add a ladle of pizza sauce to the dough and top with slices of fresh mozzarella. Finish with the chopped olives and cooked sausage crumbles.

Transfer pizza to the hot pizza stone on the grill and cook for about 7–8 minutes, until the crust turns a golden brown and the cheese is melted and begins to caramelize.

Slice into six to eight pieces and serve hot.

Tip

Pre-grilling ingredients, like sausages, peppers, onions, and other vegetables, while the grill is heating up to pizza-stone temperature is a great way to make quick work of this dinner assembly.

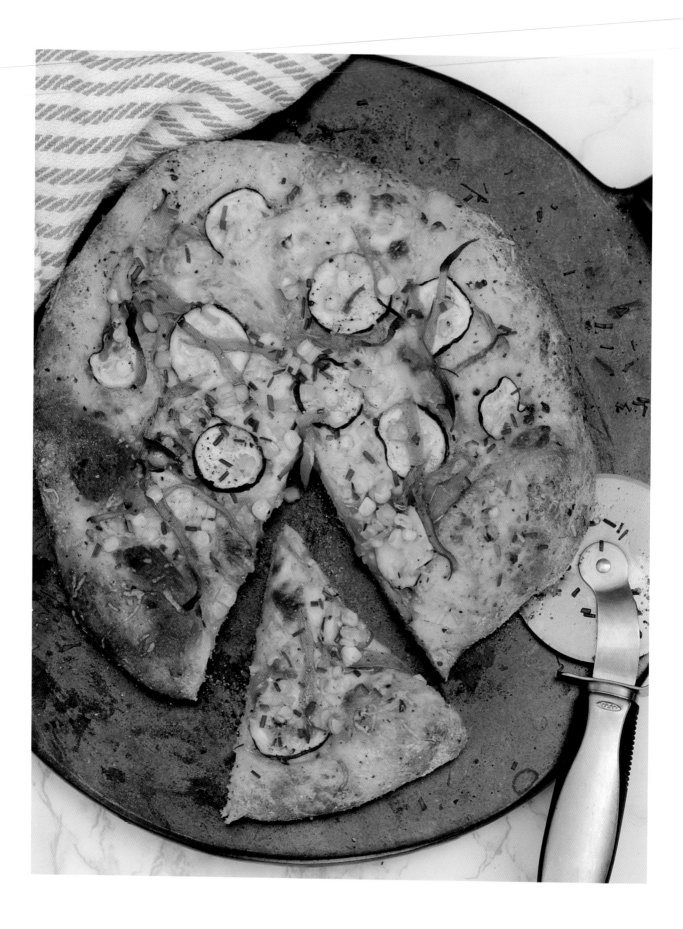

Grilled Summer Vegetable Pizza

1 PIZZA, SERVES ABOUT 4

I like to create a few menu options. Stick with a classic cheese pizza for one option, offer another classic with a meat-based topping like pepperoni, sausage, or meatballs, and include a vegetarian option as a third choice. When summer vegetables are at their best, I like to use fresh and colorful options straight from the farm stand. Grilled corn kernels, ribbons of bright orange carrots, and thinly sliced rounds of zucchini are a few of my favorite ideas for a summer vegetable–inspired pizza.

Get creative with the toppings you find in season, and experiment with other flavors like summer squash, grilled eggplant, or different mushroom varietals. With any of the vegetable toppings, the key is to prepare them so they cook evenly and quickly on the pizza by pre-grilling the ingredients, or by slicing them thin and small enough that they'll cook quickly under the grill's high heat.

INGREDIENTS

1 ear of corn
1 large carrot
1 small zucchini
Homemade Pizza Dough (see page 89)
Cornmeal
Pizza Crust Seasoning (see page 90)
Olive oil
¼ cup shredded mozzarella
¼ cup shredded sharp provolone
Fresh chives, minced, for garnish

INSTRUCTIONS

Char the ear of corn on the grill as it begins to preheat to 500°F. Place the pizza stone on the grill to heat up for 20 minutes.

Prepare the vegetable toppings: Remove the kernels of grilled corn from the cob, use a vegetable peeler to slice ribbons of carrots, and thinly slice the zucchini.

On a baking sheet, lightly dust a layer of cornmeal to prevent the dough from sticking. Stretch the dough into a 12- to 14-inch circle.

Season the pizza dough with your pizza crust seasoning spices.

Drizzle the pizza dough with olive oil and top with a combination of shredded mozzarella and provolone cheeses.

Top the pizza with the prepared vegetables, layering corn, carrot ribbons, and zucchini slices.

Transfer pizza to the hot pizza stone on the grill and cook for about 7–8 minutes, until the crust turns a golden brown and the cheese is melted and begins to caramelize.

Slice into six to eight pieces, garnish with finely minced fresh chives, and serve hot.

Grilled Goat Cheese and Tomato Pizza

1 PIZZA, SERVES ABOUT 4

The great thing about pizza is that you can eat it for every meal of the day. Yes, even breakfast! I make a breakfast pizza with crumbled breakfast sausage, crisp green scallions, a drizzle of hot sauce, and fried eggs cooked right on top. Pizza for lunch and pizza for dinner are no-brainers. I even make pizza as an appetizer too! This grilled pizza recipe with goat cheese, provolone, and sweet roasted tomatoes works well as an appetizer option because it skips the red sauce in favor of a drizzle of olive oil. The combination of cheeses holds the toppings on firmly so that you can grab a small slice and not worry about a mess as you mingle at a party.

INGREDIENTS

Cornmeal
Homemade Pizza Dough (see page 89)
Pizza Crust Seasoning (see page 90)
Olive oil
¼ cup goat cheese crumbles
¼ cup shredded provolone
3 tablespoons grated Parmesan cheese
1 cup Roasted Tomatoes (see page 95)
Fresh herbs (parsley, chives), for garnish

INSTRUCTIONS

Preheat grill to 500°F. Place the pizza stone on the grill to heat up for 20 minutes.

On a baking sheet, lightly dust a layer of cornmeal to prevent the dough from sticking. Stretch the dough into a 12- to 14-inch circle.

Season the pizza dough with your pizza crust seasoning spices.

Drizzle the pizza dough with olive oil and top with goat cheese crumbles, shredded provolone, and grated Parmesan cheese.

Top the pizza with the prepared roasted tomatoes, spread evenly over the surface.

Transfer pizza to the hot pizza stone on the grill and cook for about 7–8 minutes, until the crust turns a golden brown and the cheese is melted and begins to caramelize.

Slice into six to eight pieces, garnish with finely minced herbs, and serve hot.

Autumn

OYSTER SHUCKING PARTY MENU

Raw Oysters and Accompaniments

Classic Cocktail Sauce

Simple Mignonette

Grilled Lemon Garlic Shrimp

Grilled Corn on the Cob
Served Street Corn–Style with Herbed Aioli

Roasted Potatoes
With Maple Dijon Vinaigrette

Spicy Bloody Mary Mix
For a Build-Your-Own Bloody Mary Bar

AS SUMMER SHIFTS TO AUTUMN, THERE IS A BRIEF PERIOD OF RATHER WARM DAYS THAT ROLL INTO CHILLY, CRISP EVENINGS. It's my favorite time of year to entertain outside without the heavy summer heat. This time of year calls for a casual, seafood-inspired lunch served with grilled menu items, ice-cold spicy Bloody Marys, and tons of fresh oysters.

Oysters were formerly a rather intimidating delicacy to me, and the process of shucking them at home was even more intimidating. Once I gave them a try though, I was hooked. Trying new varietals has become a bit of a hobby. In fact, I keep a running "oyster list" of all the oysters I've tried, including type, flavor notes, and location, and a score out of 10. My favorite oysters have deep brine and tend to be from Maine, Prince Edward Island, Wellfleet Cape Cod, or the South Shore of Massachusetts (where I live!).

My absolute favorite oysters, the 10 out of 10s on my list, are from Island Creek Oyster Farm in Duxbury, Massachusetts. Local access to oysters as delicious as these meant we had to learn how to enjoy them at home. I make my husband do the shucking (because I'm a bit accident-prone), while I prepare the ice-filled serving dish and all of our condiments and accompaniments. I'm also great at mixing up a cocktail or opening an icy local IPA for us to enjoy while he does all the hard work.

A light meal of grilled shrimp, charred corn on the cob with a flavorful aioli, and rustic roasted potatoes in a maple-Dijon vinaigrette is perfect alongside fresh oysters. Each dish is easy to prepare in advance and cook up quickly so that we're spending more time digging into raw oysters and sharing drinks than working in the kitchen.

KNOW YOUR OYSTERS

Selecting Your Oysters. There is an old saying about oysters that they should only be eaten during months with the letter "r" in their names. You can actually eat oysters year-round thanks to modern oyster farming and refrigeration. But because of the lifecycle of the oyster and the impact of colder waters, oysters do tend to taste best in cooler months. Purchase your oysters from a reputable seller, and ask them questions about where they came from and what their flavors are like. Look for shells that are closed tightly and feel heavy. Plan to shuck and eat them soon after. Fresh is best!

Shucking Your Oysters. Opening up those tasty oysters takes a little bit of work, but the muscle is worth the reward! Start by cleaning the oysters; scrub them well under running cold water to wash away any mud, sand, or shell grit. Discard any open oysters that do not close to the touch.

One side of the oysters will be flat and one side more concave; place the oyster on a kitchen dishtowel with the flat side up. Use the kitchen towel to protect your hand and locate the hinge at the pointed end of the oyster. Insert the tip of the oyster knife into the hinge and twist and pry the knife to loosen the top shell and pop it open. Lift away the top shell and run the knife along the bottom to loosen the oyster from the shell. Try not to spill the juices inside the shell; the briny liquid is one of the best parts of eating an oyster!

Serving Your Oysters. As you shuck your oysters, place them on a large rimmed dish filled with ice to keep them chilled before serving. Plan on serving them right after they've been shucked; make it an interactive experience for guests and shuck them outside so that everyone can watch! Alongside the oysters you may want to include a mignonette or cocktail sauce, freshly cut lemon wedges, or some hot sauces for topping. You can also add other seafood elements to the plate, like shrimp cocktail for dipping in your homemade cocktail sauce.

Classic Cocktail Sauce

SERVES 8–12

Grabbing a jar of cocktail sauce for your seafood is totally fine, but I promise you that after you find out how easy it is to make your own, you'll never want the grocery-store stuff again. In fact, I'd bet that you have almost all the ingredients in your refrigerator and pantry right now. I personally like having a homemade cocktail sauce because it allows me to adjust the spiciness levels with additional horseradish and hot sauce. We live in a more-heat-the-better household, and the extra kick in the cocktail sauce is perfect for our collective spice-loving palate. The recipe I've shared here has a mild, low level of spice; you can taste-test and add more as needed.

Oyster purists may scoff at the scoop of cocktail sauce I spoon onto the shell before I slurp into the briny delicacies, but I love how the sweet and spicy elements of the sauce combine with the salty oysters. I also use this cocktail sauce recipe when I'm serving shrimp cocktail at a party; the sauce was made for dipping chilled shrimp into for that extra burst of flavor. You can make the sauce ahead of time and keep it in the fridge for about a week.

INGREDIENTS

½ **cup chili sauce**

¼ **cup ketchup**

3 **tablespoons prepared horseradish**

1 **tablespoon lemon juice**

2 **teaspoons Worcestershire sauce**

½ **teaspoon Tabasco sauce (add more for spicier sauce)**

½ **teaspoon Old Bay Seasoning**

INSTRUCTIONS

Combine all the ingredients in a small mixing bowl and thoroughly stir to incorporate seasonings.

Taste cocktail sauce and adjust for spiciness level; add more horseradish and Tabasco sauce if desired.

Chill for at least 30 minutes before serving.

Simple Mignonette

SERVES 8-12

A mignonette is a sauce traditionally served with raw seafood, made with minced shallots, cracked pepper, and vinegar. The mignonette has an acidic, mouth-puckering bite to it that complements the cold fresh oysters. I add a dash of wine to my recipe and a bit of fresh parsley for an herbal flavor and bright color. When serving oysters, offer your guests this vinegar-based condiment alongside the more sweet and tangy cocktail sauce, with fresh lemon wedges and some hot sauce too.

INGREDIENTS

2 tablespoons minced shallots

1 tablespoon minced fresh parsley

1 tablespoon white wine

⅓ cup red wine vinegar

1 teaspoon freshly cracked black pepper

INSTRUCTIONS

Combine the finely minced shallots and parsley in a small bowl. Add white wine and vinegar, and season with freshly cracked black pepper; stir to combine all the ingredients.

Refrigerate at least 30 minutes before serving.

Tip

If you follow the basic ratios of shallots, vinegar, and black pepper, you can make numerous combinations of mignonette flavors. Experiment with different types of vinegar to create different bases; champagne vinegar, white wine vinegar, and apple cider vinegar will all produce a variety of new sauce flavors. You can also mix in a dash of sugar for a sweeter spin, fold in other types of herbs like chives or scallions for more onion flavors, or zest citrus into the mignonette for a fresh tartness. Some restaurants will even freeze the mignonette and serve it as a granita-style slush to drop on the raw oysters before eating—try it at home!

Grilled Lemon Garlic Shrimp

SERVES 6-8

Grilled shrimp is a perfect dish for entertaining—all the prep work can be done in advance, and they cook in less than ten minutes on the grill.

The shrimp marinade has the acidic fresh citrus and garlic flavors that pair so well with grilled seafood flavors, and just a hint of paprika for a fragrant peppery note. Be sure to soak wood or bamboo skewers in water for a few hours before grilling so they don't burn.

Shrimp taste best when grilled quickly at a high, direct heat. I make it a point of not leaving the grill once the shrimp are on and cooking, so grab any cooking tools and serving plates you'll need before you get them on the hot grill. Once they're done, I like to do the hard work of sliding them off the skewers and finishing them with fresh scallions, so that guests can easily spoon a few of the charred shrimp off the platter and onto their plates.

INGREDIENTS

- 2 pounds raw shrimp (Jumbo size, 20-25 shrimp per pound)
- ¼ cup olive oil
- Juice of ½ lemon
- 2 garlic cloves, minced
- 1½ tablespoons minced fresh parsley
- 1 teaspoon paprika
- 1 teaspoon cracked black pepper
- 2 tablespoons chopped fresh scallions

INSTRUCTIONS

Prepare shrimp: Remove shells, rinse, and pat dry.

In a bowl, combine olive oil, lemon juice, minced garlic cloves, fresh parsley leaves, and paprika to create the shrimp marinade.

Toss the shrimp in the olive oil mixture and let them rest in the marinade for about 1 hour.

Remove the shrimp from the marinade and thread them on skewers; season with freshly cracked black pepper.

Heat your grill to medium-high heat for about 10 minutes, then add the shrimp skewers directly onto the grill grates.

The shrimp will cook quickly, about 2–3 minutes per side. Flip the shrimp skewers as soon as you can see the first side turning pink along the edges.

When the shrimp become opaque and char lines appear, quickly remove them from the grill and let them rest on a plate for 2 minutes.

Remove shrimp from the skewers and transfer to a platter; toss the shrimp with fresh scallions before serving.

Grilled Corn on the Cob

Served Street Corn–Style with Herbed Aioli

SERVES 6-8

"Mexican Street Corn" is having a moment, combining sweet grilled corn with salty cotija cheese grated finely across the hot kernels, and finishing it off with a Mexican crema. With corn being so bountiful and juicy in New England, even through the end of August and into September, I thought this dish deserved a Northeasterner's take.

I grill the corn naked for those eye-catching charred, nutty kernels, and tie back some of the husks for a built-in handle (and an A+ on presentation). Then I top the hot corn with those essential fine crumbles of cotija cheese, and finish it off with an aioli packed with citrus, garlic, and herbs.

INGREDIENTS

For Herbed Aioli

1 cup mayonnaise

2 tablespoons lemon juice

1 teaspoon Dijon mustard

2 garlic cloves, minced

1 tablespoon minced parsley

½ teaspoon paprika

½ teaspoon black pepper

For Grilled Corn on the Cob

6-8 ears of corn

Cotija cheese

Herbed aioli

INSTRUCTIONS

Prepare aioli by combining mayonnaise, freshly squeezed lemon juice, Dijon mustard, minced garlic cloves and parsley, paprika, and black pepper in a bowl. Stir to combine, and set aside in the refrigerator until ready to serve.

Husk the ears of corn, leaving a few pieces of husk intact at the base of the corn. Use a discarded piece of the cornhusk to tie the remaining husk strands back to make a handle.

Remove all corn silk strands and set corn aside on a tray until ready to grill.

Preheat grill on high heat for 15 minutes to get the grates nice and hot, and then place your corn directly on the grill. Rotate each ear of corn every 3–4 minutes, rotating about one-third of the way each time.

When all sides are charred from the grill, about 10–15 minutes, remove the corn from the grill and transfer to a serving platter.

Grate cotija cheese directly onto the hot grilled corn and drizzle with the herb aioli; finish with additional parsley and paprika for color if desired. Serve remaining aioli on the side.

Tip

Grill corn ahead of time to make this dish a salad for a large group. Use a sharp knife to remove the corn kernels and transfer them to a bowl. Mix in a bit of grated cotija cheese, aioli, and more fresh herbs for a festive and flavorful corn salad.

Roasted Potatoes
With Maple Dijon Vinaigrette
SERVES 6-8

With a menu of light, fresh seafood filled with hints of bright citrus and deep ocean brine, you can work in a heartier side dish like roasted potatoes. Baby red potatoes are my favorite variety to use because of their waxy texture and flavorful skin that puckers under the high heat of the oven. After roasting the potatoes until they've softened and started to brown, they're tossed in vinaigrette, which adds flavor and almost caramelizes on the outside. Maple syrup, spicy mustard, and onion-flavored bursts from shallots and scallions give this staple potato dish some complex flavors. The vinaigrette also stands well on its own; make a double batch and use it to dress a bowl of mixed greens to serve alongside these dishes. The potatoes taste delicious hot out of the oven, but also serve well at room temperature, which makes for a great entertaining dish that can be prepped and cooked ahead of guests arriving.

INGREDIENTS

3 pounds small red potatoes

1 large shallot

Salt and black pepper

For Maple Dijon Vinaigrette

4 tablespoons olive oil

3 teaspoons maple syrup

3 teaspoons brown mustard

1 teaspoon apple cider vinegar

6 dashes of Worcestershire sauce

1 tablespoon diced scallions, plus more for garnish

INSTRUCTIONS

Preheat oven to 425°F.

Wash the potatoes and cut into uniform pieces: quarter and halve larger potatoes, leave smaller potatoes whole. Transfer the potatoes to a rimmed baking sheet.

Thinly slice the shallot and disperse the slices over the potatoes.

Season the potato and shallot mixture with salt and pepper, and roast in the oven at 425°F for 45 minutes.

While potatoes are roasting, prepare the vinaigrette. In a mason jar, combine olive oil, maple syrup, brown mustard, apple cider vinegar, Worcestershire sauce, and diced scallions. Vigorously shake the vinaigrette in the sealed mason jar to combine the ingredients.

Remove the potatoes from the oven after 45 minutes and toss them with the prepared vinaigrette. Return the tray to the oven for an additional 5–7 minutes.

Garnish with additional freshly diced scallions before serving.

Spicy Bloody Mary Mix

For a Build-Your-Own Bloody Mary Bar

A Spicy Bloody Mary is my absolute favorite daytime cocktail. They are a delicious addition to a brunch menu, and make for a delightful pairing when served at luncheons where seafood is highlighted, like in this menu. Making homemade Bloody Mary mix is just a matter of shaking up a bunch of ingredients and chilling them in a large pitcher, but that little bit of effort makes a big difference in flavor. I also like to be able to control the heat in the mix; additional prepared horseradish and hot sauce make for a spicier drink, which is my favorite part of a Bloody Mary. Serving these drinks is all about presentation; after you concoct the mix to your liking, take some time to set up your bar with tons of garnishes so guests can DIY an over-the-top cocktail.

INGREDIENTS

2½ cups tomato juice

1 tablespoon prepared horseradish

1 tablespoon lemon juice

1 teaspoon olive brine

1 teaspoon juice from jarred pepperoncini

1 teaspoon Tabasco sauce

½ teaspoon Worcestershire sauce

½ teaspoon freshly cracked black pepper

¼ teaspoon celery salt

INSTRUCTIONS

In a large pitcher, add tomato juice, prepared horseradish, and lemon juice; stir to fully incorporate horseradish. Add olive brine and pepperoncini juice. Reserve the olives and pepperoncini for garnishing.

Season with Tabasco sauce, Worcestershire sauce, freshly cracked black pepper, and celery salt. Stir to combine, then taste to adjust spiciness to your liking; add additional horseradish or Tabasco sauce to increase spice and heat.

Serve over ice with vodka and garnishes such as celery stalks, lemon or lime wedges, fresh seafood like lobster claws or shrimp cocktail, or spears of olives, pickles, and peppers.

Build a Bloody Mary Bar

Basic Bloody Mary Recipe. To mix up your own Bloody Mary, pour 1.5 ounces of vodka over ice and top with about 4 ounces of the Bloody Mary mix; shake to combine and serve in a pint glass with festive and flavorful garnishes. Other variations on the traditional Bloody Mary have different types of liquor; try replacing vodka with white tequila and swap the lemon juice for freshly squeezed limes.

Flavor Glass Rims. Add a flavored rim to the edge of your Bloody Mary glass for a professional presentation. Run a slice of lemon or lime around the edge of the glass to create a damp, sticky ring around the rim. Then dip the top of the glass in a salt and pepper rim seasoning. Swap in Old Bay, celery salt, or other seasonings to customize your flavors.

Traditional Garnishes. Part of the fun of a Bloody Mary is the well-adorned glass full of colorful garnishes. Traditional garnishes include wedges of lemon and lime, spears of olives, and long, crunchy celery sticks.

Over-the-Top Additions. The possibilities for taking your Bloody Mary garnish to over-the-top status are endless. I once ordered a Bloody Mary that had a crispy, deep-fried hash brown on a skewer sticking out of the top of the glass! A few more fun ideas for garnishing Bloody Marys: crispy caramelized pieces of bacon; seafood skewers with shrimp cocktail or lobster tails; cheese-stuffed olives, pickled peppers, or spicy pepperoncini; or spears of sharp cheeses cut into bite-size cubes.

FALL HARVEST
PORCH PARTY MENU

Pumpkin Butter
Served with Brie and Pecans

Autumn Root Vegetable Soup
Served with Toasted Pepitas

Mac and Cheese Baked Apples

Butternut Squash Stuffed Pork Loin
Served with Roasted Brussels Sprouts

Apple Cider Bourbon Punch

Mason Jar Apple Pies
With Homemade Pie Dough

SUMMER BRINGS THE RHYTHM OF COOKOUTS AND LONG WEEKENDS THAT ARE CONSTANT CAUSE FOR CELEBRATION. The winter months have what seems like a continual beat of flagship holidays. Stuck in between is a quiet little time slot in the fall when we are content to have a moment to gather ourselves and enjoy some slow time at home with family. I think that may be why fall is my favorite season. The calendar full of obligations lightens up, and we can spend our weekends combing through the apple orchard, crunching leaves on chilly walks, and gathering friends and family *just because*.

Autumn is, I think, the most wonderful time to live in New England. We live in a coastal town, and as the vacationers head home, life near the water continues on, just with a few more layers of clothing. We venture out on the weekends to find the perfect pumpkins and gourds for our front porch. We visit the orchards and gather ingredients for comforting harvest cooking. We warm up with a strong drink and sit out on our patio, with the sun working against the brisk air, and hold our ground on outdoor entertaining until the very last second of the season slips away. Entertaining outdoors in the fall isn't for everyone, but I find that New Englanders are a hearty bunch.

My mother has provided me with years of inspiration for autumn porch parties. We grew up in a well-loved Victorian house right on the main street of a quaint little village. The house, which we lovingly called "Sixty-Two Bedford," had an open-door policy for friends and family and guests. On any given evening, the back door would swing open and a family friend passing through would be invited to pull up an extra seat

for dinner. The house's location, right near the center of town, meant that we had a prime viewing location for the annual firefighter's parade and carnival. My mom threw the biggest party for the occasion and invited everyone she knew. I mean *everyone*. If you saw her in the grocery store during the weeks leading up to the event, you'd surely garner an invite. This magical night is where my love for the porch party is rooted—kids tumbling around on the lawn, family perched on the porch bannisters with drinks in hand, and friends grabbing some casual bites of food while mingling on the front steps.

The key to the porch party is setting up your bar outdoors. It sets the tone for guests that we're taking this party outside the house, so grab your jacket and pour yourself a drink! It's a great solution for entertaining if you live in a small space. There is the added bonus that your drinks will generally stay chilled in the brisk autumn air. Bring a table outside to hold a signature cocktail, a few bottles of wine, and a cooler below with beer and sodas. In the fall months, I love to make a core-warming punch with a bourbon or whiskey base as my cocktail.

The other occasion where our front porch was full of life was on Halloween night. There were high-traffic sidewalks filled with trick or treaters in our cozy little neighborhood, and our house served as home base for our friends and their parents. My mom would treat the evening as an open-house-style party and make a big pot of chili or a warm harvest-inspired soup and leave it on the stove all night. Friends would pop in and fix themselves a bite, imbibe in some Halloween brews, and catch up on the porch as kids flowed up and down the street in their costumes.

The principles of the Halloween porch party still hold true when I entertain today; the evening is all about casual, easy to grab bites with warm harvest flavors. The inspiration for this menu came from those parties and is full of autumnal flavors without much fuss. I start with a robust cheeseboard, overflowing with charcuterie, dried fruits, nuts, and seasonal spreads for guests that are popping in and out during an open-house setting. Warm, creamy soup made from root vegetables and seasoned with cumin and cinnamon takes a page from my mom's book—having a pot of soup on the stove makes for a very welcoming vibe. And hearty fall dishes like roasted pork loin and rich mac and cheese have a stick-to-your-bones effect on a chilly autumn day. The season comes alive in a menu full of apples, butternut squash, pumpkin, and other flavors that are so quintessentially autumn.

How to Build a Better Cheeseboard

Pick a Base. Start at the bottom, the bottom of your cheese plate, that is. When building a large cheeseboard for entertaining, I love to use a big marble pastry board, because the marble is sturdy and stable and, most importantly, stays cool and keeps the cheeses and meats from warming up too quickly in a room full of guests. If you don't have a marble board, try a large piece of slate or an oversize wooden cutting board.

Cheese Selections. Most entertaining experts will tell you that a good cheeseboard has one hard cheese, one soft cheese, and one crumbly cheese like a blue cheese. I'm here to tell you that a good cheeseboard has whatever kind of cheese you and your family likes—throw out the rules! I love pungent, rich blue cheese, but whenever I put it on a cheeseboard, it's always the one cheese that no one touches and I end up throwing out—and wasted cheese is no laughing matter.

I recommend starting with approachable cheeses, like sharp cheddar and a creamy brie or Camembert. Then add one or two more cheeses that might be a bit more flavorful or adventurous. A goat cheese rolled in herbs or seasonal dried fruits can be delicious. Manchego, Gouda, Havarti, and gruyère are a few of my other favorite cheeses that I use often when entertaining.

Something Salty. Once you have your cheese selections down, add a few salty ingredients to your board. During cooler months a selection of charcuterie can be a delicious and savory complement to the cheeseboard. Peppery salami, thinly sliced pieces of prosciutto, and spicy pepperoni make great choices. Another route for adding saltiness to your cheeseboard is through a variety of nuts; fill some small bowls with a selection of nuts and nestle them onto the board in between your cheeses.

Something Sweet. To balance the saltier components of the cheeseboard, add a few sweet elements too. Fresh or dried fruit, like juicy grapes and dried apricots, can add color and texture. Smooth and sweet spreads, like a fig jam or pumpkin butter, spread on crackers and paired with cheeses are another delicious addition to the cheeseboard.

Crackers, Breads, and Toasts. A cheeseboard without crackers is a lonely sight. Your guests will want something to spread the cheeseboard ingredients onto, so fill in the board with a selection of crackers, breads, and toasts in a variety of sizes and textures. I like to pick at least one or two crispy crackers and balance them with a softer element like a fluffy baguette or pita toasts.

Garnishes and Greens. The key to finishing off your cheeseboard like a pro is with garnishes. Drizzle one of the softer cheeses with local honey, fill in any gaps on the plate with dried fruit, and tuck in fresh green herbs like rosemary sprigs for a final pop of color and aroma before serving.

Pumpkin Butter
Served with Brie and Pecans
SERVES 12

An easy way to make a rustic cheeseboard feel a bit more seasonal is to pair your cheeses and accompaniments with a sweet homemade fruit spread. Fig jam is one of my favorite cheeseboard spreads in the winter months, and I use a sweet local honey for spring flavor pairings. In the fall though, I love bringing in the flavors of the season with a rich, sweet pumpkin butter. It simmers on the stove and thickens into a delicious sweet spread that complements creamy brie and nuts wonderfully; I also love how the flavor plays off saltier charcuterie and cheeses on the platter.

INGREDIENTS

1 (15-ounce) can pumpkin puree

⅓ cup apple cider

½ cup granulated sugar

1 tablespoon honey

1 tablespoon maple syrup

1 teaspoon cinnamon

½ teaspoon ground nutmeg

Brie cheese, crackers, and candied pecans, for serving

INSTRUCTIONS

In a small saucepan, combine pumpkin puree, apple cider, sugar, honey, maple syrup, cinnamon, and nutmeg.

Bring mixture to a boil and then lower temperature to simmer for 45–55 minutes, until it reduces and thickens.

Remove from heat and set pumpkin butter mixture aside to cool completely.

Serve with cheese, crackers, and candied pecans.

Tip

This recipe makes a great hostess gift if you're attending a party in the cool autumn months. If you double the recipe to make an extra batch to gift, it may need a bit longer to cook and reduce—about 65–70 minutes. Portion the pumpkin butter out in small jars and share it with a bag of candied nuts and artisan crackers for a simple homemade gift.

Autumn Root Vegetable Soup
Served with Toasted Pepitas
SERVES 4-5

A hearty autumnal soup is pure comfort in my book, and often an unexpected item for guests when entertaining. If you're hosting a more formal dinner party, I love the idea of starting with a soup because it's so easy to make in a big batch and serve plated with eye-catching garnishes. For larger open-house-style parties, a rich and filling soup is an inexpensive way to feed a crowd. You can keep the soup warm on the counter in a crockpot on the warming function, or leave it on the stove at a low simmer in a large dutch oven. Place a tray of all the fixings on the side, like roasted pepitas, a swirl of crème fraîche, a few fresh herbs, and rustic crusty bread.

This recipe doubles and triples easily with no modifications, so you can make a giant batch to serve for a party, or keep it to a weeknight dinner portion for your family and make the recipe as is.

INGREDIENTS
½ butternut squash (about 3 cups)
2 medium parsnips (about 1 cup)
5-6 carrots (about 1½ cups)
1 apple
½ yellow onion
Olive oil
½ teaspoon cinnamon
½ teaspoon cumin
Salt and black pepper
3 sprigs fresh rosemary
3 sprigs fresh thyme
3 sprigs fresh sage
2¼ cups chicken broth
½ cup heavy cream
¼ cup pumpkin puree
Pepitas and bread, for serving

INSTRUCTIONS
Preheat oven to 425°F.

Prepare the vegetables: Peel and cube the butternut squash and parsnips, peel and slice the carrots, and peel and quarter the apple and onion.

Arrange vegetables on a rimmed baking sheet; drizzle with olive oil and season with cinnamon, cumin, salt, and pepper.

Add the fresh herbs on top of the vegetables and roast at 425°F for 55–60 minutes, until vegetables are softened.

Remove fresh herb sprigs and transfer the roasted vegetable mixture to a blender. Pulse until the mixture breaks down and starts to become smooth.

Add chicken broth, heavy cream, and pumpkin puree to the blender and pulse until smooth.

Transfer soup to a dutch oven on the stovetop and simmer to keep warm for serving. Garnish with pepitas and fresh herbs, and serve with rustic crusty bread for dipping.

Tip

If you're hosting a formal dinner party and want to impress your guests, make this recipe as a roasted root vegetable puree to use when plating your entrees. Reduce the amount of chicken broth you put in the blender by approximately half. Then place a dollop of the puree on a plate and use the back of the spoon to spread it out in a fan shape before placing your protein (like the Butternut Squash Stuffed Pork Loin on page 136) on top.

Mac and Cheese Baked Apples

SERVES 6

When my husband and I got married and went on our honeymoon, we decided to drive across the country. Much of the trip was spent exploring restaurants in different cities, one of our favorite activities to do together. One of the most memorable meals from the trip was from a small eatery in Cleveland where I ordered mac and cheese off the menu. When it arrived, piping hot in a ceramic dish, the waiter also dropped off a bowl of homemade applesauce. I was perplexed since I didn't order applesauce, but the server instructed me that the chef served the two together so that guests could dip the mac and cheese in the applesauce. I gave it a try and it was amazing. It made sense; after all, I'd heard of people serving apple pie with slices of sharp cheddar cheese.

When I returned home from the honeymoon, I was ten pounds heavier and full of inspiration gathered on our culinary cruise across the states. One of the first items on my brainstorm list was how to take this apple and cheddar pairing to the next level. I have worked for years to perfect my homemade mac and cheese recipe, and decided to bake this classic dish inside a hollowed-out apple for an edible serving vessel. These mac and cheese apples are a showstopper on a buffet table and seem to garner excitement from kids and adults alike.

Pick large, firm red apples for this recipe. I like Empire apples because they're particularly round, which makes hollowing them out to hold the pasta a bit easier. I also like to test the apples on a flat surface at the grocery store to make sure they'll stand up well on a serving dish—some apples are too round at the bottom and can roll away. Pick ones that will stand up well when you bake and plate them.

INGREDIENTS

6 cups cooked pasta (elbows or medium shells)

6 large red apples

3 tablespoons butter

3 tablespoons flour

1¼ cups heavy cream

1 teaspoon Dijon mustard

3 tablespoons Parmesan cheese

2½ cups shredded cheddar cheese, divided

¼ teaspoon onion powder

¼ teaspoon garlic powder

Salt and black pepper

INSTRUCTIONS

Preheat oven to 425°F.

Cook pasta as directed; drain and set aside.

Using a sharp knife, slice off the top ½ inch of the apple to create a flat top. Scoop the inside of the apple out, removing the core and some of the inner apple. Leave about ¼ inch of the apple intact to maintain the structure of the fruit when it's baked.

Repeat with the remaining five apples and arrange them in a baking dish.

In a pot, melt the butter over medium heat and whisk in the flour, cooking until combined and thickened to create the base of the cheese sauce.

Whisk in the heavy cream, Dijon mustard, and Parmesan cheese and cook over medium heat for about 3 minutes.

As the sauce starts to thicken, stir in 2 cups of the shredded cheddar cheese, onion powder, and garlic powder. Continue to stir until all the cheese is melted into the sauce.

Remove from heat and fold in the cooked pasta. Coat with the cheese sauce and season with salt and pepper to taste.

Divide the mac and cheese among the six apples and top with the remaining cheddar cheese before baking at 425°F for 20 minutes.

Tip

Serving a larger crowd? You can easily skip the apples and make this mac and cheese recipe as a casserole instead. Follow the instructions above for the mac and cheese, doubling the measurements for larger servings, and bake in an oven-safe dish for 15 minutes, about 5 minutes less than you would inside the apples. Extra cheese and buttery panko bread crumbs make a delicious topping for the mac and cheese when baked in a casserole dish; also consider mixing in fresh peas or roasted butternut squash cubes for added flavor and texture.

Butternut Squash Stuffed Pork Loin

Served with Roasted Brussels Sprouts

SERVES 8

The stuffing mixture is the star of the show in this roasted pork loin recipe, with sweet roasted butternut squash bits combined with nutty pecans and fresh sage. The corn bread binds it all together and adds lots of depth to the flavor. Slicing into the roasted pork after it rests is sort of like opening up a present, exposing the surprise of delicious swirls of stuffing inside. I serve the slices over a bed of roasted brussels sprouts; it's an eye-catching entree for autumn entertaining.

INGREDIENTS

4-pound boneless center cut pork loin

1½ cups cubed roasted butternut squash

1½ cups corn bread crumbs

1 yellow onion, minced

1½ tablespoons butter, melted

½ cup chopped pecans

2 tablespoons minced sage

Salt and black pepper

Roasted brussels sprouts, optional, for serving

INSTRUCTIONS

Preheat oven to 450°F.

Prepare pork loin by trimming excess fat and then butterflying the loin open with a sharp knife. Unroll the meat and slice the remaining edges of the loin that are still thicker than the open center, until the pork loin is lying open and flat on a cutting board. Pound the pork loin with a meat tenderizer mallet until the whole thing is an even thickness, about ½ inch tall.

Prepare the stuffing by combining the roasted butternut squash cubes with crumbled corn bread, minced onion, melted butter, and chopped pecans.

Fold in the minced sage leaves to the stuffing mixture and season with salt and pepper.

Spread the stuffing mixture across the tenderized pork loin in a thin even layer, pressing it down so that it sticks to the surface. Roll the meat like a jellyroll to secure the stuffing inside.

Use butcher's twine to tie the rolled pork together in 2-inch intervals, until the whole loin is securely tied. Place in a rimmed baking dish and season with salt and pepper.

Roast the pork at 425°F for about 60 minutes, until the internal temperature reaches 140–145°F.

Remove from oven and let it rest for at least 15 minutes before slicing. Remove strings and slice to serve.

Apple Cider Bourbon Punch

SERVES 10-12

A big-batch cocktail is one of my favorite ways to serve a specialty drink. For starters, it's a good excuse to buy a festive drink dispenser to dress up your bar cart. It's also a great way to let guests serve themselves without the work of mixing a complicated cocktail. My favorite perk of a punch, though, is that you can mix all the ingredients together before the party (minus the ice) and have it ready to serve and refill without much effort.

This punch is packed with seasonal flavors. Fresh, local apple cider from the orchard is such a treat to use in a drink like this. (I like to use picking up the cider as an excuse to swing in and grab a few warm apple cider donuts while I'm there too.) The cider and ginger flavors mix with the bourbon for a core-warming cocktail that is perfect to enjoy on a chilly fall afternoon while sitting on the porch.

If you don't have a drink dispenser, use a large trifle dish as a punch bowl, or divide the punch into smaller batches and serve in pitchers or carafes. I also like to leave a bit of extra apple cider and ginger beer on the side, without bourbon in it, as non-alcoholic options for guests.

INGREDIENTS

6 cups apple cider
2 cups bourbon
Juice of ½ lemon
1 (12-ounce) bottle ginger beer
Ice
1 apple
Cinnamon sticks

INSTRUCTIONS

Pour apple cider, bourbon, lemon juice, and ginger beer over ice in a large drink dispenser or punch bowl. Stir the ingredients together to combine.

Thinly slice one apple horizontally to create apple discs; float them in the drink dispenser on top of the ice.

Serve punch over ice with whole cinnamon sticks as a flavor-infusing garnish.

Mason Jar Apple Pies

With Homemade Pie Dough

SERVES 8

Apple picking is a bit of a must-do when the weather changes to that brisk fall air in New England. Once my quilted barn coat comes out of the closet for the season, I feel a gravitational pull toward the apple orchards. We pull on our boots and head out down the long rows of trees, branches bowing under the weight of all their shiny red and green fruit. Once we've gotten our share of family pictures in the orchard and have a heaping bag full of freshly picked fruit in tow, we head home and scratch our heads about what exactly we're going to do with all these apples.

Applesauce for the kids, apples stuffed with mac and cheese for dinner, apples sliced and nibbled on with cinnamon and peanut butter—oh, and of course apples baked into the dessert of the season: apple pie. My grandmother's apple pie might be the first recipe I ever cooked alongside her. It's a childhood rite of passage to roll out homemade pie dough with Grandma while balancing on a step stool to reach the counter.

For a modern spin on the classic apple pie, bake the filling inside small mason jars. Each jar gets a whole crisp Granny Smith apple, cooked down with spices and sugars, and then is topped with flaky fresh pie dough discs. You can get creative with the pie dough toppings and cut out letters to assign a pie to each guest on the guest list, or add seasonal shapes like fall leaves with cookie cutters. I opted for a simple pie dough heart on top of these, to let my family know they were baked with love (and lots of butter).

INGREDIENTS

For Pie Dough
2¼ cups all-purpose flour
½ teaspoon salt
1 teaspoon granulated sugar
1 cup (2 sticks) cold butter
⅓ cup cold water

For Apple Filling
8 Granny Smith apples
1 cup granulated sugar
1½ teaspoons cinnamon
1 teaspoon nutmeg
½ teaspoon mace
1 teaspoon cornstarch
1 teaspoon flour
2 teaspoons lemon juice

INSTRUCTIONS

To make pie dough, sift together flour, salt, and sugar in a large bowl. Cut the cold butter into small pieces (or shred on a large box cheese grater quickly while it's still very cold). Add the butter to the flour mixture and work the two together until crumbly. Add the cold water slowly and continue to work with your hands until the dough is crumbling and starting to come together.

Don't overwork the dough; as soon as it starts to come together, divide into two portions and roll into discs. Cover in plastic wrap and transfer to the fridge to chill for at least 1 hour.

To prepare the filling, peel, core, and slice eight Granny Smith apples and transfer to a bowl. Toss the apples with sugar, spices, cornstarch, flour, and lemon juice.

Transfer to a saucepan and cook the apple mixture for about 5 minutes, until the apples start to soften.

Preheat oven to 350°F. Divide and spoon the filling evenly into eight 8-ounce wide-mouth mason jars on a rimmed baking sheet.

Remove the pie dough from the fridge and roll out to ½-inch thickness; cut out eight 4-inch round discs.

Place the discs over the top of the mason jar openings and press down around the sides of the rim. Use any leftover dough to create decorative toppings to finish the jar pies.

Bake at 350°F for 25–30 minutes, until you can see the apple filling bubbling and the pie-crust finish to a golden brown. Let the jars cool before serving, as the glass will be hot coming out of the oven.

NEW ENGLAND THANKSGIVING DINNER MENU

Thanksgiving Turkey

Sweet Potato Stuffed Mushrooms

Brussels Sprouts Salad
With Shallots and Dried Cranberries

Maple Dill Roasted Carrots

Parmesan Chive Mashed Potatoes

Skillet Apple Sausage Corn Bread Stuffing

Brown Butter Pumpkin Ravioli

Pecan Pie Ice Cream Sundae Topping
Served with Vanilla Bean Ice Cream

Spiced Orange-Cranberry Simple Syrup
Sparkling Prosecco Cocktail

THANKSGIVING WAS ALWAYS ONE OF MY FAVORITE HOLIDAYS GROWING UP. I loved the fact that we got to stay in our pajamas until the late morning, snuggled up on our living room couch watching the Macy's Thanksgiving Day Parade. My Mom would yell, "Girls! It's the Rockettes!" as our favorite high-kicking dancers graced the screen, and we'd run to stand far too close to the screen to absorb all the magic of the parade. We also had the privilege as children to never have to travel far for Thanksgiving dinner. My grandparents lived on the same block as us, so close you could almost smell the gravy simmering on the stove as we made the brief walk down the street for our holiday feast.

I have to think that everyone grows up thinking that his or her own Thanksgiving is what a "traditional" Thanksgiving dinner looks like. It wasn't until I was an adult, spending Thanksgiving with my in-laws, that I realized the homemade mac and cheese served to picky eaters at my house was not actually a dish made by pilgrims at the first Thanksgiving. That is part of the fun of this holiday though. We create so many memories around the dishes that grace the holiday table that the food itself becomes a character in our story. It's not Thanksgiving without my dad making a joke about needing to be served a piece of Grandma Ida's apple pie as soon as the meal is over. It's not Thanksgiving without my husband's uncles huddled around a turkey fryer in the freezing cold. And it's certainly not Thanksgiving without inquiring minds asking just how many sticks of butter I managed to get in the mashed potatoes. (The answer is always: *You don't want to know.*)

Tradition is certainly an important part of this celebration. I'd never dare mess with the sanctity of Grandma's pie recipes. For every classic dish on the table though, I do love to try new twists on Thanksgiving favorites. I'll happily put a scoop of classic box-made stuffing on my plate right next to my fancy apple-sausage-corn bread version. Like with family and friends during the holiday season, I like to think the more the merrier: around the table *and* on my plate.

LET'S TALK TURKEY

Buy the Bird. It's almost time for Thanksgiving and you've got to pick up the centerpiece of the feast: The Turkey. Estimate about 1 pound of turkey per guest, or a bit more if you're passionate about lots of leftover turkey sandwiches. We're lucky to live close to some turkey farms that offer farm-fresh turkeys around the holidays, but most turkeys you purchase for Thanksgiving are going to be frozen. It can take quite a long time for a turkey to properly thaw, so plan ahead. Place it in its wrapper on a rimmed baking sheet in the fridge and assume the bird will need approximately 24 hours for every 4 pounds of weight to thaw.

Brine Time. There are massive forums on the Internet that debate the effectiveness of brining a turkey. Dry brine versus liquid brine, what flavors to add to your brine, how long to brine for—it's a rabbit hole of passionate discussions. I've grown accustomed to using a traditional liquid brine, so that's my vote in this heated debate. Why should you brine your turkey? The brine helps the turkey retain moisture while cooking and helps season the meat of the bird more deeply. About 24 hours in advance of cooking the turkey, fill up a brining bag with 1 cup salt, 1 cup sugar, ½ cup whole black peppercorns, and about six bay leaves. Put the turkey into the bag with the brining seasonings, fill the bag with water to fully cover it, and let the whole thing hang out in a roasting pan in your fridge.

Cooking the Bird. An hour or two before you're planning on starting to cook the turkey, remove it from the fridge and give it a rinse to remove any of the brine left on the outside. You want to do this because the sugar left on the skin could burn in the oven and you'll end up with charred skin. After it's fully rinsed, pat the whole thing dry with paper towels and get ready to add lots of herbs and butter to the outside and under the skin for a juicy, flavorful turkey.

It's this time of year that I remember how unreliable oven calibrations can be, so consider buying an oven thermometer that sits inside the oven to accurately tell you how hot it is in there. I am always shocked to see how far off my oven is if I don't let it preheat long enough. Your turkey and piecrusts will thank you!

You'll want to cook your turkey in the oven at around 350°F, and estimate about 13–15 minutes of cooking for every pound of turkey. Turkeys that have stuffing inside them will take longer to cook. The turkey is done when the internal temperature of the breast meat reaches 165°F.

The Deep-Fried Option. I love the visual of a big turkey coming out the oven in a piping hot roasting pan on Thanksgiving. Sometimes though, a fried turkey is a great option if you're serving a ton of people and need to cook more than one bird. There's only so much room in the oven, and moving some turkey cooking outside can help free up space! I fried a turkey once and it came out delicious—juicy and crispy and a beautiful golden color. I also felt like the process took years off my life because I was so nervous about fires and accidents. If you do fry a turkey, pay extra attention to ensure that the bird is thoroughly thawed, rinsed, and dried to avoid those oil-splattering incidents.

The Presentation. The turkey is essentially the centerpiece of the whole Thanksgiving dinner (which I find unfair; we all know the stuffing and mashed potatoes are the Best Supporting Actors that *should* have won the Oscar). With this high-stakes responsibility on the holiday buffet line, the turkey deserves the best presentation possible. When you finish cooking the turkey, let it rest for about 30 minutes before cutting into it, to allow the juices to be absorbed back into the meat. After it cools, transfer it to your serving platter and fill in around the turkey with greenery. I like to use leftover herbs like bunches of sage leaves and rosemary and thyme sprigs. You can also nestle in some cut citrus like halved oranges or brightly colored persimmons or pomegranates for a really festive look.

Tip

I've used this same stuffed mushroom concept to use up lots of other Thanksgiving leftover sides. Try stuffing mushrooms with leftover mashed potatoes, stuffing, or squash and baking them in the oven to create a brand-new appetizer for entertaining over the holiday weekend.

Sweet Potato Stuffed Mushrooms
SERVES 6-8

This recipe, while a delicious appetizer or side dish to serve at Thanksgiving dinner, was actually inspired by using up post-holiday leftovers. I decided to take a few of the leftover side dishes from our Thanksgiving dinner and experiment with them as fillings in a spin on classic stuffed mushrooms. The final version I'm sharing here has a filling made of mashed sweet potatoes with butter and brown sugar, chopped-up mushrooms, and some prepared stuffing. It gets mixed together and scooped into mushrooms caps that are baked in the oven to warm and soften and crisp.

I use portabellini mushrooms, which are small portabellos that measure about two to three inches in diameter. This size is great for serving as a side dish if you estimate one to two mushrooms per guest. If you plan to make the stuffed mushrooms and serve them as an appetizer, consider using an even smaller mushroom, like baby bellas that are one to two inches in diameter for bite-size scale.

INGREDIENTS

12 mushroom caps (2–3 inches in diameter)

1½ cups mashed sweet potatoes

1 tablespoon brown sugar

1 tablespoon butter

2 tablespoons chopped fresh flat leaf parsley, plus more for garnish

1 cup prepared stuffing

Salt and black pepper

INSTRUCTIONS

Preheat oven to 400°F.

Clean the mushrooms with a damp cloth, removing any dirt or grit. Remove the stems from the mushrooms and discard. Use a spoon (a melon baller works great) to partially hollow out the inside of the mushroom. Reserve the scraped mushroom pieces in a bowl and place the hollowed-out mushroom caps in a rimmed baking dish.

In a bowl, combine mashed sweet potatoes with brown sugar and melted butter. Stir until sugar and butter are fully incorporated into the potatoes.

Roughly chop the reserved mushroom pieces; fold mushrooms and parsley into the sweet potato mixture.

Add the prepared stuffing to the sweet potato mixture and stir to combine the ingredients. Add salt and pepper to taste.

Scoop the sweet potato filling into the hollowed-out caps until all the mushrooms are stuffed. Estimate about 2–3 tablespoons of filling per mushroom cap.

Bake the stuffed mushrooms at 400°F for about 30 minutes. During the last 2 minutes of cooking time, turn the broiler on to crisp the tops of the mushrooms.

Garnish with additional fresh parsley before serving.

Brussels Sprouts Salad
With Shallots and Dried Cranberries
SERVES 6-8

I didn't grow up in a salad-for-Thanksgiving household. The only green you'd see on our table was hidden under French's crispy onion rings in a highly caloric green bean casserole. One year at a Friendsgiving party I was attending, someone was assigned to bring the salad and a lightbulb went off in my head: What if instead of a "green" salad, we made a crispy brussels sprouts salad? They're green, and it's still a salad, so it checks all of the boxes but is so much more flavorful. You get punches of salty bacon, sweet dried cranberries and shallots, and then the crispy crunch of the brussels sprouts; it's a hearty dish that can stand up to the rest of the indulgent sides on your Thanksgiving dinner plate.

INGREDIENTS
6 cups brussels sprouts
4-5 thick slices bacon
1 tablespoon olive oil
⅓ cup thinly sliced shallots
⅓ cup dried cranberries
Salt and black pepper

INSTRUCTIONS
Preheat oven to 450°F.

Prepare brussels sprouts by cleaning, trimming, and thinly slicing them into ¼-inch pieces. Transfer to a large rimmed baking sheet.

Heat a skillet and cook the bacon slices until crispy; remove from pan and set aside to cool. Reserve the bacon fat from the pan.

Toss the brussels sprouts, olive oil, and sliced shallots together on the baking sheet with the reserved bacon fat from the pan.

Roast the brussels sprouts mixture at 450°F for 15 minutes.

While the brussels sprouts are cooking, chop the bacon into small pieces.

Remove the pan from the oven and toss the crispy brussels sprouts with the bacon and dried cranberries, then return to the oven for an additional 5 minutes to heat through before serving. Season with salt and pepper to taste.

Maple Dill Roasted Carrots

SERVES 6

Have you ever noticed how a Thanksgiving dinner plate can look sort of color-less? The tastiest things are all shades of neutral brown and beige: gravy, stuff-ing, potatoes. Of all days of the year, this isn't exactly one where I feel the "eat your vegetables" notion should take priority, but I do believe a plate should have a pop of color! Some families add the customary bright orange hue on the plate with sweet potatoes, others with butternut squash, but I love the texture and flavor of carrots next to my turkey. This version gets flavor from the sweet and earthy combination of maple syrup and freshly chopped dill.

INGREDIENTS

1½ pounds carrots

3 tablespoons butter

3 tablespoons maple syrup

Salt and black pepper

1 tablespoon minced fresh dill

INSTRUCTIONS

Preheat oven to 450°F.

Peel carrots and cut them into uniform pieces, about 3–4 inches long. Place the carrots on a rimmed baking sheet.

In a small saucepan, combine the butter and maple syrup and heat until just melted.

Toss the carrots in the butter and syrup mix-ture on the baking sheet. Season with salt and pepper.

Roast the carrots at 450°F for 30 minutes. Turn the broiler on for the final 2 minutes of cooking.

Remove from the oven and toss with freshly minced dill; taste and season with additional salt and pepper if needed.

Tip

To get fluffy mashed potatoes, use either a potato ricer or a hand masher. I prefer a few bites of non-mashed bits in my potatoes for texture, so a hand masher has always been my preference. A potato ricer will give you a smoother-textured mashed potato. Don't use a blender or food processor to mash the potatoes though; they'll end up gluey!

Parmesan Chive Mashed Potatoes

SERVES 6-8

Mashed potatoes are what I would call my signature Thanksgiving dish; it's the side that I always get assigned to bring when we celebrate the holiday with my family. I suppose this is because I'm quite passionate about the state of the potatoes and just don't trust that anyone else will put quite enough butter in them. One of the greatest food compliments that I've ever received is praise from my dad that my mashed potatoes were on par with his own grandmother's. My great-grandmother Katherine was a bit of a spitfire, from what I've heard, and made some darn good mashed potatoes. I'd like to think this compliment gave me some kitchen-related confidence that may have eventually pushed me down a path to write about food, so thanks for that, Dad.

My secret mashed potatoes ingredients are a bit of sour cream for a tangy taste, Parmesan cheese for some savory depth, and freshly chopped chives for color and flavor. I also put tons of butter into the potatoes when I make them, and usually have extra on hand to fold into the potatoes as they're getting warmed and ready to serve. You can never *have enough butter. I also use red potatoes in this recipe because I like a bit of texture to my potatoes; if you want very smooth potatoes, you may want to opt for a russet potato instead.*

INGREDIENTS

3 pounds red potatoes

10 tablespoons butter (plus more for melting on top)

¼ cup heavy cream

¾ cup sour cream

½ cup Parmesan cheese

½ cup minced fresh chives

Salt and black pepper

INSTRUCTIONS

Scrub the potatoes well and remove any grit from the skin.

Bring a large pot of salted water to a boil. Drop uncut, skin-on potatoes into the boiling water.

Cook the potatoes for about 25–30 minutes; remove a potato and test for doneness. A knife should glide easily through the potato when they're cooked through. Large potatoes may need more time to cook, so test different sizes.

Drain the cooked potatoes and transfer to a large bowl, then add butter chopped into small cubes to the potatoes to melt while they're still hot.

Use a hand masher to begin to mash the potatoes and incorporate the melting butter. After butter is melted, add in the heavy cream and sour cream.

Mash until you reach your desired texture and then fold in the Parmesan cheese and fresh chives, and season with salt and pepper to taste.

Serve hot with additional butter melted over the top and more fresh chives.

Tip

The cast-iron skillet actually makes a difference in the outcome of this recipe, as it adds lots of flavor when you cook and bake it in the same dish. You don't lose out on any of the crispy little bits of shallots and sausage at the bottom of the pan. The added bonus is that when you cook and serve it in the same pan, you have one less dish to do after dinner! If you don't have a cast-iron skillet, cook as directed in a large pan and transfer the stuffing to a baking dish to finish in the oven and get the desired crispiness on top.

Skillet Apple Sausage Corn Bread Stuffing

SERVES 6-8

Stuffing is the most delicious food on earth. There, I said it. For some reason we only make it on Thanksgiving, which I suppose is what makes it so special. I'd be delighted to see stuffing making its way into everyday meals though, because it's worthy of enjoying a few more times a year. Even the boxed version is great, but I promise my fancy dressed-up homemade version is worth a try.

I love the flavors that come through from juicy bites of apple, caramelized shallots, and, of course, the corn bread. The whole thing comes together in a cast-iron skillet and looks so lovely and rustic coming out of the oven and going right onto the table. Just a few sprigs of thyme are all it needs before you dig in.

INGREDIENTS

2 (8-ounce) boxes corn bread mix

3 sweet Italian sausages

½ cup (1 stick) butter, divided

1 large yellow onion, chopped

2 shallots, thinly sliced

2 red apples, skinned, cored, and cubed

2 cups chicken stock

¼ teaspoon celery salt

½ teaspoon black pepper

1 tablespoon minced fresh thyme, plus sprigs for garnish

INSTRUCTIONS

Prepare the corn bread as directed and leave out uncovered overnight.

Preheat oven to 450°F.

Remove the sausage from its casing and cook in a large cast-iron skillet until all the small crumbles are browned; remove and set in a large bowl.

In the same skillet, melt 4 tablespoons of the butter and add the chopped onions, thinly sliced shallots, and cubed apple pieces. Sauté

until onions begin to soften; remove from pan and add to sausage.

Add the chicken stock to deglaze the skillet, scraping up any remaining onions. Cook until the stock is warmed.

In the large bowl containing the sausage and onion mixture, add celery salt, pepper, and minced thyme leaves.

Cube the stale corn bread and add to the bowl; toss all the ingredients together.

Slowly pour the warmed chicken stock over the corn bread mixture and begin to combine. Use 1½–2 cups of the stock, depending on how dry your corn bread was to start.

Transfer the corn bread stuffing back to the skillet. Melt the remaining 4 tablespoons butter and drizzle over the corn bread.

Bake the stuffing in the skillet at 450°F for 15 minutes. Garnish with fresh thyme leaves.

Brown Butter Pumpkin Ravioli

SERVES 4-6

My family has a few members that aren't exactly vegetarians (they're not big fans of vegetables), but they don't really participate in the turkey eating at Thanksgiving time either. You might call them carb-eterians? In order to accommodate for a few guests that don't eat turkey, we usually have one vegetarian pasta dish on our Thanksgiving menu. Oftentimes it's my classic mac and cheese recipe that finds its way to the table, but another dish that works well with these autumnal holiday flavors is this brown butter pumpkin ravioli.

Homemade ravioli is a delicious option, but with all the other cooking going on for the holiday, I usually rely on some freshly made ravioli from the store. The sauce comes together very quickly and combines browned butter, crispy sage leaves, a bit of sweetness from the pumpkin puree and just a touch of brown sugar, and nuttiness from nutmeg and Parmesan cheese. It's an indulgent pasta dish that always impresses guests, and tastes so good I even sometimes make it for a weeknight dinner!

INGREDIENTS

20 ounces fresh ravioli

5 tablespoons butter

6 large fresh sage leaves, thinly sliced

1 tablespoon brown sugar

¼ teaspoon grated nutmeg

⅔ cup pumpkin puree

¼ cup chicken broth

½ cup reserved pasta water

¼ cup grated Parmesan cheese

Freshly cracked black pepper

INSTRUCTIONS

Boil water and cook ravioli as directed to al dente doneness; reserve ½ cup of the pasta water.

In a saucepan, combine butter with thinly sliced fresh sage leaves over medium heat and cook until butter browns and begins to foam.

Add brown sugar, nutmeg, and the pumpkin puree to the butter mixture and whisk to fully combine until sugar is dissolved.

Whisk in the chicken broth and reserved pasta water to loosen sauce, and continue to cook until heated through.

Toss in the cooked ravioli and coat the pasta with sauce; finish by tossing with Parmesan cheese and freshly cracked black pepper.

Pecan Pie Ice Cream Sundae Topping

Served with Vanilla Bean Ice Cream

SERVES 6-8

Growing up, we had two pies at the end of Thanksgiving dinner: apple and pumpkin. Imagine my surprise when I found out, later in life, that there is a whole wide world of pies beyond these two flavors. I always look forward to the rich, sweet, and nutty flavors of a pecan pie now; it's a dish that is perfect for holiday indulgences. When it comes to pecan pie though, I really just want more of the good stuff—that syrup-coated sweetness of crunchy toasted nuts. I got to thinking: What if I just made the filling and ate it on its own? Of course a big bowl of pecan pie filling is borderline excessive, even for the holidays. So I made it anyway and found it to be the perfect topping for vanilla ice cream, which makes it a totally reasonable dessert—not excessive at all.

My pecan pie sundae topping gets its flavor from good vanilla extract, sweet brown sugar and maple syrup, a bit of bourbon, and a dash of sea salt. It really does taste delicious on its own, but scoop it over vanilla ice cream to be a bit more civilized about the whole thing. Quality, locally made vanilla bean ice cream is worth the splurge—it makes a big difference in taste. We buy ours from a farm located a few towns over and make an event out of it. My daughter gets to say hi to the cows, and we fill up our basket with their baked goods, fresh dairy products, and lots of their homemade ice cream.

INGREDIENTS

2 cups whole pecans

⅔ cup brown sugar

¼ cup maple syrup

4 tablespoons (½ stick) butter

2 tablespoons dark corn syrup

1 tablespoon bourbon

1 tablespoon vanilla extract

1 teaspoon sea salt

INSTRUCTIONS

In a saucepan, lightly toast the pecans for 2 minutes on medium heat.

Add brown sugar, maple syrup, butter, dark corn syrup, bourbon, vanilla extract, and sea salt to the pecans in the saucepan.

Cook for 10 minutes over medium heat, stirring frequently.

Remove the pan from the stove and let sauce cool for 15 minutes at room temperature before serving over vanilla bean ice cream.

Spiced Orange-Cranberry Simple Syrup
Sparkling Prosecco Cocktail
SERVES 12

At Thanksgiving dinner, a nice big glass of red wine is probably the best choice to pour as you sit down to a heaping pile of turkey. Before the feasting starts though, I think a festive holiday occasion is the best time to pop a bottle of bubbly and clink glasses to all that you're thankful for. To make that bottle of prosecco a little more festive, adding a seasonal spiced orange-cranberry simple syrup is a lovely touch. It brings loads of flavor to your bar cart with the tartness of the cranberries, bright orange citrus, and wintry anise and clove spices. The colors pop too; adding some orange slices and fresh cranberries in small bowls for drink garnishes do double duty for both drink and holiday decor.

INGREDIENTS

1 cup water

1 cup granulated sugar

1 cup fresh cranberries, plus more for serving

2 oranges, plus more for serving

1 anise pod

4–5 whole cloves

Prosecco, for serving

INSTRUCTIONS

In a saucepan, combine water and sugar with cranberries and bring to a boil.

Quarter the oranges and add them to the liquid mixture along with the anise and cloves.

Lower heat and bring the syrup to a simmer; cook for 35–40 minutes, until reduced by half.

Strain the liquid into a pourable container, removing the cranberries, orange pieces, anise, and cloves. Squeeze any remaining liquid out of the fruit before discarding.

Cool the syrup completely before adding to chilled prosecco. Garnish drinks with orange slices and fresh cranberries.

Thanksgiving Leftover Ideas

If Thanksgiving is the quintessential family feasting holiday, then the day after Thanksgiving must be the official day of leftovers. I actually Googled it, the official National Leftover Day seems to exist, and of course it's celebrated in late November. I love the creative challenge of finding new ways to use leftovers after turkey day, and have a few favorites from my experiments:

Mashed Potato Breakfast Burritos. I had the most delicious breakfast burrito of my life in Austin, Texas, and it was because of the savory potatoes mixed in with the eggs. I like to re-create this handheld breakfast bite with leftover Thanksgiving mashed potatoes. Add a scoop of potatoes to a frying pan and warm them up with freshly cut scallions, a bit of sharp cheddar cheese, and fluffy scrambled eggs. Roll them up in warmed flour tortillas and serve with hot sauce.

Corn Bread Stuffing Hash. My dad taught me to appreciate a creative breakfast hash and I've made this one for him the morning after Thanksgiving. While hash is usually made with potatoes, I like to use leftover stuffing in this post-holiday breakfast recipe. Any stuffing will work, but I think it tastes especially good with my corn bread-sausage stuffing recipe. Chop up a few onions, scallions, and toss in the leftover stuffing on a skillet with some oil and crisp up the leftovers until it becomes a hash-like texture. Serve it with a fried egg on top; a runny egg yolk is a must.

Thanksgiving Pot Pie. The best bite of Thanksgiving dinner is when you manage to get a little bit of every single element of the feast on your fork. I make a leftover potpie creation that ensures every slice tastes like that perfect bite from Thanksgiving dinner. Use leftover pie dough to line a pie dish and layer in chopped leftover turkey, a drizzle of gravy, a layer of mashed potatoes, more gravy, stuffing, and then a spread of cranberry sauce into the dish. Top it off with more piecrust and bake it at 350°F until bubbling hot and golden brown (about 35 minutes) and serve it with more gravy.

Winter

CHRISTMAS EVE OPEN HOUSE MENU

Spicy Cheddar Chive Pub Cheese
Served with Sourdough Pretzels

Spinach Artichoke Pastry Wheels

Apple Walnut Baked Brie
With Green Apple Slices and Crackers

Holiday Green Salad
With Cranberry-Orange Vinaigrette

Baked Sweet Potatoes
With Goat Cheese, Dried Cranberries, Walnuts, and Sage

Christmas Penne a la Vodka
With Spicy Sausage and Spinach

Sugared Cranberries
With Reserved Cranberry Syrup

IF YOU ONLY ENTERTAIN ONE TIME A YEAR, I'LL BET THAT IT'S AT CHRISTMAS. It's the peak of entertaining season, with cookie swaps and ugly sweater parties and holiday brunches and, of course, Christmas Eve and Christmas Day celebrations, entrenched with traditions that last for years and years, passed down to each new generation.

My family makes a big deal about Christmas Eve. It's a jam-packed day of parties, eating, and spending time with friends and family. We start in the afternoon at our family friend's house for an open-house-style party, with guests coming and going before they head off to visit family or attend church. It is, without a doubt, my favorite holiday ritual.

What I love about this party is the tradition. The homemade linzer tart cookies are always in the same spot on the dessert buffet, a crockpot of the host's meatballs are always warming on the corner of the kitchen island, and at the end of the night all the "kids"—*yes, I'm in my thirties*—still get a chocolate Santa from a basket by the door as we put on our coats and head to the next event. There is some serious Christmas magic that goes into hosting a big gathering like this, and I'm so grateful that they do it every year to keep the beloved tradition alive.

After the party we make our way home for Christmas Eve dinner. It's a bit of a challenge to create dinner for a big group when everyone is spending the afternoon at various other holiday parties. Over the years, we've had to curate a menu that can be mostly prepared ahead of time, but still feels festive and celebratory. We all descend on the house around 5:30 p.m., and as the coats are coming off and wine is being opened, it's time to entertain.

This Christmas menu is designed for that very same holiday whirlwind we experience every year with our family, when you're both a guest and a hostess in the same day. You need small appetizer bites that can be pushed out quickly to keep guests busy while you're putting the final touches on the meal, self-serve cocktails that your family can mix and pour themselves, and dishes that can be mostly prepared in advance so that you can make quick work of getting dinner on the table.

If you can do most of the cooking and prep work in advance of hosting the dinner, you'll only need about thirty to forty minutes in the kitchen to get everything on the table. It's the perfect amount of time to let family arrive, pour themselves a holiday cocktail, and mix and mingle before you sit down to celebrate the season together.

Christmas Menu Prep

Prep the Bar. Make the sugared cranberries the day before, reserve the simple syrup, and set wine and champagne chilling.

Make-Ahead Appetizers. Make the pub cheese a day before the party, set it in the fridge to chill, and wait to add fresh chives until right before serving. Prepare the spinach artichoke pastry wheels a day or two in advance, and slice and bake when you're ready to serve. Assemble and chill the apple walnut baked brie in the morning, and cook it in the oven when you get home.

Get a Head Start on Dinner. Precook the sweet potatoes in the morning, portion out all the toppings, and then just reheat them in the oven and do final assembly when you're ready to serve dinner. Prep the salad and cover with plastic wrap in the refrigerator. Make the salad dressing in advance and dress the salad right before dinner is served. Brown the sausage in the morning for the pasta; add it back to the pan to start the sauce while the pasta cooks.

Spicy Cheddar Chive Pub Cheese

Served with Sourdough Pretzels

SERVES 8

In the late afternoon when everyone is visiting for the holidays and ready for a happy hour (the holidays are about spending time with your family; a little afternoon cocktail never hurt anyone), my mom always asks if anyone wants a little "nosh" as we twist open bottles of wine and get pouring. It's an occasion where a full appetizer spread isn't really necessary, but a few little snacks make their way out onto the ottoman in the family room while we relax. Pub cheese is a staple that's always on hand for these casual occasions.

This homemade version has tons of flavor from the sharp cheese, heat from hot sauce and horseradish, and a touch of freshness in the chives. It's addictive, and goes so well with crispy sourdough pretzels. I like to double the batch and put a few portions of it in tiny mason jars to give as hostess gifts and bring to parties around the holidays. It's also a great snack for a Super Bowl party too; make a batch of homemade soft pretzels to pair with it for an impressive gameday snack.

INGREDIENTS

2 cups shredded sharp white cheddar

1 cup shredded mild yellow cheddar

2 ounces cream cheese

¼ cup IPA beer

3 tablespoons sour cream

1 tablespoon Worcestershire sauce

1 teaspoon Dijon mustard

1 teaspoon hot sauce (or more, to taste)

½ teaspoon prepared horseradish

1 garlic clove

1 teaspoon paprika, plus more for garnish

Black pepper

2 tablespoons minced fresh chives

INSTRUCTIONS

In a food processor bowl, add shredded cheeses, cream cheese, beer, sour cream, Worcestershire sauce, Dijon mustard, hot sauce, horseradish, garlic, and paprika. Blend to combine all the ingredients until smooth.

Taste and season with black pepper and more hot sauce if needed; pulse to incorporate into the pub cheese.

Fold in 1 tablespoon minced fresh chives and transfer the pub cheese to a serving bowl.

Garnish with remaining 1 tablespoon fresh chives and additional paprika before serving with sourdough pretzels, crackers, or carrots and celery.

Spinach Artichoke Pastry Wheels

SERVES 24

I have an actual problem with spinach artichoke dip. The problem is I can't stop eating it. If it's in front of me, in a big warm bread bowl, I lose every ounce of self-control. I don't eat it; I inhale it. This recipe was inspired by the savory, rich dip in an effort to help me pace my spinach artichoke dip intake.

It starts with the very same base that I use for a spinach artichoke dip and gets spread in a thin layer across puff pastry sheets. The puff pastry gets rolled up into spirals, with a bit of the filling peeking through in every layer, and then sliced into bite-size wheels. When they bake, they puff up into pretty little pinwheels, flecked with green bits of spinach, which look festive for the holiday season.

Homemade puff pastry is certainly delicious, but the frozen puff pastry works so well and the differences are negligible. When you're buying the frozen variety, look on the label for an all-butter puff pastry for the best flavor.

It's quick work to make the filling for these pastry wheels in a food processor, but if you don't have one you'll be fine! Finely chop the spinach, artichokes, scallions, and garlic by hand before combining with the rest of the ingredients. Use the back of a fork to mash the mixture together and fully incorporate the cream cheese (softened, room temperature cream cheese works best).

INGREDIENTS

4 sheets frozen puff pastry dough

2 cups frozen spinach

⅓ cup artichoke hearts

2 scallions

1 garlic clove

1 teaspoon fresh lemon juice

1 teaspoon fresh lemon zest

4 ounces cream cheese

¼ cup mayonnaise

¼ cup Parmesan cheese

1 teaspoon paprika

Salt and black pepper

INSTRUCTIONS

Preheat oven to 400°F. Line a baking sheet with parchment paper.

Thaw puff pastry and roll out on a lightly floured surface.

Place spinach, artichoke hearts, greens of the scallions, and garlic clove into the food processor and pulse to chop.

Add lemon juice and zest, cream cheese, mayonnaise, Parmesan, paprika, and salt and black pepper to the food processor; blend to combine. Taste and add more pepper and salt if needed.

Divide the filling across the puff pastry sheets and spread it into a thin, even layer. Spread to the edge on three sides of the pastry; leave one side with a 1-inch border free of the filling.

Tightly roll the pastry dough toward the edge without filling, finishing with the end of the pastry dough tucked underneath the roll. Press lightly to seal the end of the pastry dough to itself.

Place in the refrigerator for 15 minutes to chill before slicing into spiral discs, about ½ inch thick.

Place the discs on the baking sheet and bake at 400°F for 24 minutes, until the puff pastry has expanded and turned a light golden tone.

Remove from oven and serve immediately.

Tip

Make a large batch of these at the beginning of the busy holiday season and freeze them in their uncut rolled state. They'll last for about 2 weeks if wrapped well in plastic wrap. Remove them from the freezer and let them rest at room temperature for 15 minutes before slicing into discs and baking as directed.

Apple Walnut Baked Brie
With Green Apple Slices and Crackers
SERVES 6-8

Have you ever noticed how everyone at a party floats toward a warm, gooey baked brie as it gets set on the coffee table, like the cheese has some sort of super-strength magnetic pull? You could call it brie en croute, *if you want to be fancy, but let's call it what it is: warm, melted cheese wrapped up in flaky, buttery puff pastry. It's simple to take this favorite entertaining dish and dress it up with toppings like honey, nuts, fruit, and jams for some extra flavor and style. My favorite version has toasted walnuts and caramelized bits of apples baked on top, reminiscent of the sweet flavors of an apple pie.*

There are two tricks for making perfect baked brie. The first is to let the pastry dough thaw completely so that it is flexible and easy to work with. Handling the dough, though, can cause it to warm up, get sticky, and lose a bit of its structure. Place the wrapped brie back in the refrigerator for twenty minutes before cooking to firm the dough back up and help it retain the shape you've created with the folds of dough. The second trick is that no matter how hard it is, resist cutting into the baked brie right away. Letting it rest for about ten minutes will ensure that the cheese has enough time to firm up, while still remaining warm and gooey.

INGREDIENTS

1 sheet frozen puff pastry dough

1 (8-ounce) wheel of brie

¼ cup walnuts

2 apples

1 tablespoon butter

2 tablespoons brown sugar

2 tablespoons granulated sugar

1 teaspoon cinnamon

1 teaspoon nutmeg

¼ teaspoon sea salt

1 large egg

INSTRUCTIONS

Thaw pastry dough on a parchment paper–lined baking sheet. Cut a circle out of the pastry dough, about 10 inches in diameter, and place the wheel of brie in the center of the circle.

Roughly chop walnuts and add to a small saucepan; toast for 3–5 minutes and then remove from heat.

Peel and dice apples and add to a saucepan over medium heat with butter, brown sugar, granulated sugar, cinnamon, nutmeg, and salt. Cook for 4–5 minutes, stirring often, until the apples begin to soften and are coated with the dissolved sugar and melted butter.

Remove the apple mixture from the heat and stir in the walnuts as it cools at room temperature for about 5 minutes.

Spoon the apple and walnut mixture on top of the brie, allowing some of the pieces to spill over the sides onto the pastry dough.

Working in a circular fashion, begin to wrap and fold the puff pastry dough up around the brie, leaving some room at the top for an opening for the apple walnut mixture to show through.

Chill the assembled baked brie in the refrigerator for at least 20 minutes or up to 24 hours before preparing to bake.

Preheat oven to 400°F.

Remove brie from the refrigerator. Whisk egg with 1 teaspoon water and lightly brush the egg wash on the puff pastry.

Bake at 400°F for 30 minutes, until the pastry dough puffs up and turns a golden brown tone and the apple mixture bubbles in the center.

Let the baked brie rest for 10 minutes before serving warm with thinly sliced green apple pieces, crisp crackers, or a rustic baguette.

Tip

Looking for more delicate, bite-size appetizers? Cut the puff pastry dough into small squares and line a muffin tin with them. Fill each pastry cup with a slice of brie and a spoonful of the filling, and close the pastry dough around the top. Bake at 400°F for about 15–20 minutes, until golden brown. Guests can enjoy their own individual baked brie bite!

Holiday Green Salad
With Cranberry-Orange Vinaigrette
SERVES 6-8

Just about every year since my husband and I have lived together, I've bought a giant bag of cranberries at the beginning of the holiday season as a garnish for drinks or an ingredient in a recipe. I usually only need about a cup or so of cranberries and am left with a big plastic bag of leftover berries in the refrigerator. After a few days they make their way to the freezer because I know I'll find a use for them somewhere in my cooking experiments. Yet months after the holidays have passed, my husband invariably makes an observation about the giant bag of cranberries that I swore I was going to use taking over the freezer. It's become a running joke—the cranberries in the freezer that will never find their destiny in a future recipe.

So this holiday season, I was determined to use up those cranberries that I normally squirrel away in the back of the freezer. I candied them for garnishes to top pretty desserts. I made them into simple syrups to dress up cocktails. I baked them into breads, turned them into sauces, and yet there were still cranberries left in that bag.

This simple green salad to serve at the holidays was my solution for finally saving those last few fresh cranberries from exile in the deepest corners of my freezer. In addition to some mixed greens, I layer just a few fresh cranberries for their tartness and some dried cranberries for their sweetness. Both types of cranberries add lots of color atop bright lettuce leaves, and the red and green is perfect for the holidays! Toasted nuts for crunch, and lots and lots of creamy, rich goat cheese are layered on top (goat cheese is the quickest way to get me to eat a big bowl of salad). Finish the salad with a simple vinaigrette that comes together with sweet orange and honey notes to balance the tartness of the cranberries.

INGREDIENTS
12 ounces mixed greens
¼ cup dried cranberries
¼ cup crumbled goat cheese
¼ cup chopped toasted walnuts or pecans
2 tablespoons fresh cranberries

For Cranberry-Orange Vinaigrette
½ cup fresh cranberries
1 shallot
1 tablespoon honey
¼ cup orange juice
1 teaspoon brown sugar
½ cup olive oil
½ cup apple cider vinegar
Black pepper

INSTRUCTIONS

In a large bowl, layer mixed greens with dried cranberries, goat cheese crumbles, and roughly chopped toasted nuts. Add 2 tablespoons fresh cranberries to the top of the salad.

Prepare the salad dressing: Add ½ cup fresh cranberries to a food processor. Pulse to break the cranberries down and release their juices.

Add shallot, honey, orange juice, brown sugar, olive oil, and vinegar to the food processor and blend to combine. Season with fresh black pepper.

Dress salad immediately before serving.

Baked Sweet Potatoes

With Goat Cheese, Dried Cranberries, Walnuts, and Sage

SERVES 8

When you're planning a menu for a large group, it's always a good idea to include a vegetarian option and items that fit a range of dietary needs. One recipe that I keep in my back pocket for these occasions is a loaded baked potato. It hits two check marks: vegetarian and gluten free (with the right toppings)! You can get really creative with baked potatoes and make tons of different versions to match your menu theme. I've made Greek-style loaded potatoes with feta, hummus, dill, and chopped red onions, and I've made some with warm spinach artichoke dip spooned over the potatoes and crispy fried onions crumbled on top.

This recipe takes a wintry holiday-inspired spin and uses sweet potatoes as the base. The roasted sweet potatoes have so much flavor, they taste amazing on their own. As they come out of the oven, warm and steaming hot, drop bits of goat cheese inside to melt and soften into the potato. Sweet dried cranberries and crunchy nuts get sprinkled on top, and ribbons of fresh sage add an seasonal herbal flavor to the dish. This recipe is hearty and works as an additional main-event dish on your menu. You could also make it with smaller sweet potatoes cut into discs and serve them as a bite-size appetizer before dinner.

INGREDIENTS

4 medium sweet potatoes

4 tablespoons (½ stick) butter

Salt and black pepper

4 ounces goat cheese, crumbled

¼ cup dried cranberries

¼ cup chopped toasted walnuts

2 tablespoons chopped fresh sage leaves

INSTRUCTIONS

Preheat oven to 400°F.

Clean sweet potatoes and poke in a few spots with a fork. Place in microwave and cook for about 8 minutes.

Take cooked sweet potatoes out of the microwave and slice in half lengthwise. Use a spoon to scrape out the soft sweet potato out of the center and transfer to a bowl, reserving the skin.

Mash the sweet potatoes in the bowl with butter until the butter is fully melted and incorporated. Season with salt and pepper to taste.

Scoop the mashed sweet potatoes back into the potato skins and place on a baking sheet. Bake at 400°F for 5–7 minutes.

Remove sweet potatoes from oven and transfer to a serving dish. Top each potato half with crumbled goat cheese, dried cranberries, toasted walnuts, and chopped fresh sage leaves. Season with more salt and pepper if needed.

Tip

To prepare these in advance of your event, precook the sweet potatoes in the microwave, scoop out the center and mash with butter, and then fill the potato skins back up with the mashed sweet potato filling. Transfer the filled sweet potatoes to a baking dish, cover with plastic wrap, and refrigerate until ready to serve. Reheat the potatoes at 400°F until warmed through before finishing with toppings.

Christmas Penne a la Vodka

With Spicy Sausage and Spinach

SERVES 4-6

This Christmas pasta dish is a spin on penne a la vodka. My version is loaded with sweet shallots, tons of crumbled browned sausage bites, and wilted spinach stirred into the sauce. The red sauce with little flecks of the green spinach and parsley make up a jolly feast for the eyes. It's also a perfect dish to serve for quick entertaining, since the sauce comes together in just a few minutes while the pasta cooks.

INGREDIENTS

1 pound penne pasta

3 sweet Italian sausages

2 tablespoons butter

3 garlic cloves, minced

2 large shallots, thinly sliced

1 ounce vodka

1½ cups tomato sauce

½ cup heavy cream

½ cup packed chopped fresh spinach

½ cup Parmesan cheese, plus more for garnish

¼ cup fresh parsley, plus more for garnish

Salt and black pepper

INSTRUCTIONS

Bring a pot of salted water to a boil; cook penne as directed to al dente.

In a large saucepan over medium-high heat, remove sausage from casings and cook until browned. Crumble the sausage into small, bite-size pieces.

Once the sausage is nearly cooked through, push it to the edges of the pan and add the butter to the center. Melt the butter and add the minced garlic and thinly sliced shallots to the pan; cook until softened.

Add the vodka to deglaze the hot pan, using a spatula to scrape up any bits off the pan's surface. Cook for 2 minutes.

Add the tomato sauce and heavy cream to the pan, stirring to incorporate all the ingredients and heating the sauce through, about 4–5 minutes.

Stir in the chopped spinach, Parmesan cheese, and parsley to the sauce. Cook for an additional 3–4 minutes until the spinach is wilted into the sauce.

Add the cooked pasta to the pan, coating the penne in the sauce. Season with salt and pepper to taste.

Serve hot with additional Parmesan cheese and freshly chopped parsley garnishes.

Sugared Cranberries
With Reserved Cranberry Syrup
SERVES 12

Sugared cranberries look like little sparkly gemstones that you can magically pop into drinks, sprinkle on cheeseboards, and even use to dot the edges of a pretty vanilla cake. The tartness of the cranberries and sweet crunchy sugar coating make them so tasty, you may even just eat them on their own. They're a little hostess ninja trick that you should keep in your back pocket to bring out and impress your guests during the holiday season.

To get the cranberries to their glistening sugared state, you create a simple syrup and soak them in it overnight. The syrup infuses the cranberries and creates a sticky coating on the red skin so the dusting sugar will adhere to the outside. A little bonus result of this technique is the subtly tinted cranberry syrup left in the bowl after you scoop the cranberries out the next morning. Reserve the flavored syrup and transfer it to a small glass bottle with a pour spout so that guests can use it in their cocktails alongside the sweet sugared cranberries. The syrup and cranberries are a nice complement to a dry sparkling wine and some fresh sage leaves.

INGREDIENTS
1 cup water

2 cups granulated sugar, divided

2 cups fresh cranberries

INSTRUCTIONS
Combine water and 1 cup of the granulated sugar in a small saucepan and cook over medium heat until the sugar is fully dissolved. Remove from stove and transfer to a bowl.

Add the cranberries to the bowl of syrup and soak at room temperature overnight.

The next day, strain the cranberries from the syrup, reserving the remaining simple syrup for flavoring drinks.

In a mixing bowl, toss the strained cranberries with the remaining 1 cup sugar. Mix until all the cranberries are fully coated in sugar.

Carefully spread the sugared cranberries in a single layer on a wire cooling rack over a rimmed baking sheet.

Let the cranberries rest at room temperature for about an hour to let the sugar coating dry and firmly adhere to the cranberry skin before serving.

Use the cranberries to garnish drinks and desserts, or serve them as a snack on an appetizer or cheese platter.

Tip

Candied cranberries are so very pretty and are an easy way to dress up a box-mix or store-bought vanilla-iced cake. Use them to create a cranberry-dotted border around the base or the top rim of an iced cake, and even use a few piled up in the center with sprigs of fresh rosemary for a beautiful holiday dessert.

NEW YEAR'S DAY LUNCHEON MENU

Pear and Gorgonzola Bites
With Fresh Thyme and Honey

Mini Potato Gratin Stacks

Cheddar Chive Popovers

Herb Compound Butter

Spicy Sausage and Tortellini Soup

Chocolate Chip Cake

Lemon-Rosemary Gin Spritz

NEW YEAR'S IS MY *FAVORITE* HOLIDAY. When I say that out loud, I'm usually met with a funny response. People comment that New Year's is always overhyped and overrated, full of expensive dinner reservations, crowded bars, and overall disappointing evenings. These retorts are actually *exactly* why I love it so much. It's a holiday underdog. I love hosting a New Year's party to squash all of their bad New Year's in the past, and make a believer out of my guests. Everything about this holiday gets me excited. I love the suspense of the count-down, the world's best excuse to drink endless amounts of champagne, the romance of a kiss at midnight. Most of all, I love the fresh start of the year, like the first page of a crisp new notebook, and all the possibilities it holds.

My love for this holiday is exactly how it became "my holiday." Each of my girlfriends has claimed a holiday; we know exactly where we're spending 4th of July, whose house we go to for Friendsgiving, and where gifts will be exchanged at the annual Christmas party. New Year's Eve is my assignment! It's an annual event that has evolved and grown up over the years, just like us.

The tradition started in college, where champagne bottles (okay, $4 bottles of sparkling wine) were sprayed on the ceilings and the aftermath was left untouched until the end of the semester. Then there were the post-college tiny-apartment years where I spent Christmas money from my grandparents on plastic champagne glasses and New Year's beads and cases of cheap prosecco, and it made me feel like the world's greatest hostess. I had a kitchen the size of a closet, one cookie sheet, and an oven door that only opened up three-quarters of the way because it hit the wall in front of it, and yet the highlight of the year was hosting my friends for this festive evening in my tiny little space.

The tradition continued, and matured over the years. The plastic champagne glasses turned into real glass flutes thanks to some of my favorite gifts from our wedding registry. The prosecco gets a little bit better each year, and there's even maybe one bottle of *real* champagne popped to start the night. One year, two friends actually got engaged at the party as the clock struck midnight. I *humbly* like to remind my friends *all the time* that I'm so good at throwing parties that people sometimes spontaneously decide to spend the rest of their lives together after attending them!

When I was pregnant with my daughter, my due date was estimated to be about one week after New Year's Eve. I was convinced I could still throw this giant party within days of my due date. Why not? After much persuasion from my husband, who always magically foresees when I'm about to take on too much, I decided to mix things up and have a small dinner party instead. Days before the party, in a moment of sheer exhaustion (turns out my husband was right), I made the call to order takeout instead of cooking the dinner. I felt deflated at the time (an ironic feeling when your body is so *inflated*), like I was letting down this beloved tradition by scaling back on the decor and DIYs and menu. It turned out to be one of my favorite New Year's Eve parties yet. The format was different, but the spirit was the same. It was a night of good friends, tons of food (that I didn't have to cook), corks popping, and my husband's perfectly curated playlist on in the background. I love this party, and look forward to it all year long.

Since that dinner party we've had a baby, our friends have had kids, people have moved and bought houses and adopted dogs. Life changes every year. It's in the spirit of the holiday to note how much we've evolved over the previous twelve months, and so the party has to change with it! Babies go to bed early, dogs have to be walked, and somewhere in your early thirties you decide that sleeping on an air mattress at your friend's house is *really* unappealing. That's where my idea came from to move our annual New Year's Eve bash to a cozy New Year's Day lunch.

It's the perfect solution for continuing this holiday tradition, but now instead of watching the ball drop at midnight, we clink glasses at noon on the first day of the New Year. Our friends with kids are delighted that a party is happening in between morning and afternoon naps. The friends who still want to go out and party it up on New Year's Eve can trickle in and nurse their hangovers with a little hair of the dog and some hearty snacks and soups and sweets.

Most of this menu can be made ahead or prepared quickly in the morning, so if you did have some champagne the night before the party, you'll still be able to entertain effortlessly. It's something that I often think about when menu planning for an event. If I can reduce stress in the kitchen before guests come over, I'm always a better hostess. Pick dishes that can be made or prepared ahead of time, like the soup recipe and chocolate chip cake in this chapter. Do as much prep work in advance as you can, like pre-shredding cheese for the popovers, preparing the herb compound butter, and chilling your drinks. Select appetizers that can be prepped the night before, like the pear and Gorgonzola bites, and pair them with other dishes that bake at the same temperature in the oven, like the potato gratin stacks, so that you have everything in the oven at once. A little bit of work and coordination in advance of the party will mean that your guests will feel how relaxed you are, and you'll get to enjoy the party (and maybe a little bit of bubbly too!).

Tip

If you're short on time when entertaining, you can make the filling the night before and let it marinate in the fridge—wait to add the Gorgonzola until the morning. You can also purchase premade puff pastry cups from the freezer section and quickly fill the puff pastry with the pear Gorgonzola mixture before baking.

Pear and Gorgonzola Bites
With Fresh Thyme and Honey
SERVES 6

Puff pastry is your best friend when entertaining; it can be turned into a million different types of delicious appetizers. I'll let you in on a little puff pastry secret, too: The only reason to make it from scratch is if you find yourself as a contestant on The Great British Baking Show. Frozen puff pastry works great and will make your life easy! Grab a box from the freezer section of your grocery store and use it to create countless combinations of fluffy appetizer bites for entertaining. This version pairs the subtle sweetness of pears and honey with savory, rich Gorgonzola for a simple filling inside the pastry.

After thawing the puff pastry, cut it into small squares and press them into a mini muffin tin to create little cups to hold your filling. You can use the same concept to make a number of different types of appetizer bites. I've used this method with a brie and fig spread filling, diced apples and toasted nuts with cinnamon, or a cheddar, cream cheese, and scallion mixture. There are dozens of other combinations of sweet and savory ingredients you could try; press that frozen pastry dough in the mini muffin tins and fill them up with whatever inspires you!

INGREDIENTS
Frozen puff pastry
1 cup peeled, diced (½-inch) Bosc pears
2 teaspoons honey
1 teaspoon fresh thyme, plus more for garnish
¼ teaspoon cinnamon
¼ teaspoon nutmeg
¼ cup crumbled Gorgonzola cheese

INSTRUCTIONS
Preheat oven to 425°F. Remove the puff pastry from the freezer to thaw.

Place diced pears in a bowl and add honey, fresh thyme leaves, cinnamon, and nutmeg; toss to combine and coat the pears.

Fold the Gorgonzola cheese crumbles into the pear mixture and set aside.

Unfold the thawed puff pastry and use a sharp knife or pizza cutter to cut the pastry into twelve 2-inch-square pieces. Place the puff pastry squares in a mini muffin tin, pressing them down to create dough cups.

Fill each puff pastry–lined cup with a spoonful of the pear and Gorgonzola filling until you have twelve completed cups.

Bake at 425°F for 15 to 18 minutes, until the pastry is puffed up and a light golden brown color. Remove from oven and serve hot with a garnish of additional fresh thyme sprigs.

Mini Potato Gratin Stacks

SERVES 8–12

Everyone loves cheese and everyone loves potatoes, but they don't always look so pretty heaped in a big casserole dish. This miniature take on the concept of gratin brings all the rich, silky flavors of potatoes baked in cheese and cream, while the delicate stacks make this hearty winter ingredient look refined and gourmet. The dish works well as an hors d'oeuvre or side dish for entertaining.

INGREDIENTS

4 large russet potatoes
1 cup heavy cream
2 garlic cloves
3–4 fresh thyme sprigs, plus more for garnish
¼ teaspoon nutmeg
½ cup Parmesan cheese, plus more for garnish
½ cup shredded sharp cheddar cheese
Salt and black pepper

INSTRUCTIONS

Preheat oven to 425°F.

Scrub potatoes clean and thinly slice them into ⅛-inch-thick rounds; transfer to a large mixing bowl.

Warm the heavy cream in a small saucepan over low-medium heat, then add the garlic, thyme, and nutmeg to the pan to flavor the cream as it cooks. Be careful to watch the temperature and keep it at a soft simmer—too much heat will break the cream.

Remove the pan from the stove after 10–12 minutes; remove garlic cloves and thyme sprigs from the cream and discard.

Pour the grated Parmesan and cheddar cheese over the bowl of potatoes, season with salt and pepper, and toss to coat the potatoes with cheese and seasoning.

In a 12-cup muffin tin, layer the thin slices of cheese-coated potatoes into the cups, filling each one. Spoon about 1 tablespoon flavored cream over each potato stack and top with any remaining cheese from the bottom of the bowl of potatoes.

Bake in the oven at 425°F for 30 minutes. Turn the oven up to broil and heat for an additional 2 minutes to brown the cheese on top of the potato stacks.

Remove from the oven and let the potato stacks rest for about 10 minutes to cool and absorb any liquid left in the cups.

Use a fork or offset spatula to scoop the potato stacks out of the muffin tins and place on a serving plate. Garnish with additional fresh thyme and a sprinkle of Parmesan cheese and freshly cracked black pepper.

Cheddar Chive Popovers

SERVES 12

Oh, how I love popovers! These puffy baked treats are made in individual muffin-like tins; the eggs in the batter help them billow up over the edges of the tin to create tall, crispy exteriors and a custardy inside.

Temperature is key to make popovers truly pop. *Warm the milk, make sure the eggs are at room temperature, preheat the oven thoroughly, and heat the pan in the oven before pouring the batter into the cups. The longer you're able to rest the batter before cooking, the taller and more flavorful the results will be. Keep the oven door closed during cooking to ensure a consistent oven temperature for the popovers to reach those sky-high heights. Follow these steps and you'll have towering popovers with all the crispy texture and warm custardy bites that make them so special. Then comes the hard part: trying not to eat them all before your guests arrive.*

INGREDIENTS

3½ cups milk

4 cups flour

1 teaspoon baking powder

1½ teaspoons salt

6 large eggs, room temperature

½ cup shredded sharp cheddar cheese

1 tablespoon minced fresh parsley

1 tablespoon minced fresh chives

INSTRUCTIONS

Warm milk over low heat in a saucepan until it is warm to the touch.

Sift flour, baking powder, and salt together in a large mixing bowl.

Crack eggs into a large bowl and beat with an electric mixer for 3–4 minutes, until they become foamy.

Add the warm milk to the foamy eggs and continue to beat the mixture.

Gradually add the dry ingredients to the wet ingredients and continue to beat for about 2 minutes. Let batter rest in the bowl at room temperature for 40–60 minutes for best results.

Preheat oven to 450°F and coat a popover pan with nonstick spray.

Combine shredded sharp cheddar cheese and parsley and chives; set aside.

Put the pan in the oven for about two minutes to warm up before filling the cups three-quarters full with the rested batter. Top each cup with a sprinkle of the shredded cheddar cheese and herbs.

Bake at 450°F for 15 minutes. Turn oven down to 375°F and bake for 30 minutes longer, until popovers are risen and golden brown. Do not open the oven during the cooking process.

Remove the popovers from the oven and transfer them to a wire cooling rack to rest for a few minutes before serving.

Tip

One of the secrets to baking a great popover is letting the batter rest for almost an hour before you bake it. For that reason, I like to make the batter first thing when I get up in the morning if I'm serving them for lunch, and then move on to prepping the rest the meal. The batter can hang out on the counter while you're cooking, and you can bake them off an hour before guests arrive so they fill the house with that fresh-baked-goods aroma and come out of the oven hot for the meal.

Herb Compound Butter

SERVES 8–12

Compound butter sounds so gourmet, so fancy, right? It's really just butter with other ingredients folded into it so that it takes on a new flavor. It's hard to imagine butter being any better than it already is in its purest form, but mixing in some flavorful ingredients, like fresh herbs, can take it to the next level. This recipe calls for citrus, garlic, parsley, rosemary, and thyme to add tons of fragrant notes to the butter.

You can use this same concept, though, to make any type of compound butter. Fold in different jams and pureed berries for a sweet butter, or roasted garlic cloves or mashed roasted tomatoes for a savory butter spread. Try cilantro, cumin, and lime juice for a compound butter to pair with corn bread, or make a maple syrup and cinnamon compound butter for a sweet breakfast addition to waffles.

INGREDIENTS

½ cup (1 stick) butter
1 garlic clove
1 tablespoon minced fresh parsley
1 teaspoon minced fresh rosemary
1 teaspoon minced fresh thyme
1 tablespoon lemon juice
Freshly cracked black pepper

INSTRUCTIONS

Put butter in a small bowl and let it come to room temperature until thoroughly softened.

Finely mince the garlic clove. Add garlic and minced fresh parsley, rosemary, and thyme to the softened butter.

Add lemon juice and freshly cracked black pepper to butter.

Use the back of a spoon to mash ingredients into the butter until lemon juice is absorbed and the garlic and herbs are fully incorporated.

Transfer to a serving dish and chill for at least 20 minutes before serving.

Tip

You may be tempted to throw these ingredients in a food processor to blend them together quickly, but ignore that instinct! Mixing by hand allows you to keep all the flecks of herbs intact within the butter. Putting it in the food processor will break down the herbs so much that the butter will turn a pale shade of green and lose that pretty speckled look.

Spicy Sausage and Tortellini Soup

SERVES 6

This recipe brings together all of my favorite soup ingredients. The hot Italian sausage is the secret that adds heat to the soup and flavors the broth. It's great for winter entertaining because it's hearty and feels like a full meal instead of just a starter dish. It comes together quickly as an easy weeknight dinner too, and satisfies those comfort-food cravings on a chilly winter evening. You can prepare the soup in advance—just wait to add the tortellini until right before serving, to keep the pasta from losing the al dente firmness. Serve hot with some extra grated Parmesan cheese on the side and a basket of homemade popovers or crusty Italian bread.

INGREDIENTS

Olive oil

4 hot Italian sausage links, casings removed

1 large yellow onion

1 large shallot

3 garlic cloves

2 large carrots

2½ cups crushed San Marzano tomatoes

2½ cups chicken broth

1½ cups cannellini beans

2 cups frozen spinach

¼ cup grated Parmesan cheese, plus more for garnish

1 tablespoon chopped fresh parsley

Salt and black pepper

1 (13-ounce) package cheese tortellini

INSTRUCTIONS

In a large dutch oven, heat a few tablespoons of olive oil. Remove casings from sausage and add to the pot to cook through.

Remove browned sausage links from the dutch oven and chop into small pieces.

Chop onions, shallot, garlic, and carrots. In the same pot, sauté vegetables for 5 minutes, until softened. Add chopped sausage pieces back to pot.

Add crushed tomatoes and chicken broth to the sausage and onion mixture and bring to a boil.

Drop the cannellini beans and frozen spinach into the pot and cook for an additional 5 minutes, until heated through. Turn heat off and stir in the Parmesan cheese and fresh parsley; season with salt and pepper to taste.

In a separate pot, cook the tortellini as directed in salted boiling water to al dente. Immediately before serving, add the cooked tortellini to the soup.

Garnish with more Parmesan cheese before serving.

Chocolate Chip Cake

SERVES 8-10

Chocolate chip cake is that one family-favorite dessert that marks special occasions at our house. This cake is requested for birthday parties, it got sent to us in the mail when we were homesick college kids, and it was made by Mom when someone needed a little pick-me-up. The beloved original is written on a flour-ridden, faded recipe card that has traveled through family members' hands for years, and the tradition continues on!

What makes this cake so special? It's a real crowd-pleaser, a cake for people who say they don't really like cake. The sour cream batter gives it an addictive tangy flavor, and the sugary chocolate chip topping adds the perfect amount of sweetness. It's less messy to serve kids than traditional frosted cake. It's also the perfect dessert to make ahead of time—it actually tastes even better the next day. If you make it ahead, leave it in the pan tightly covered overnight, and cut it right before serving for the best results.

INGREDIENTS

½ cup (1 stick) butter, softened
1¼ cups granulated sugar, divided
2 large eggs
1 cup sour cream
2 teaspoons vanilla extract
2 cups flour
1½ teaspoons baking powder
1 teaspoon baking soda
1 (12-ounce) package chocolate chips

INSTRUCTIONS

Preheat oven to 350°F. Lightly grease a 9- x 13-inch baking dish.

In a large bowl with an electric mixer, cream together softened butter, 1 cup of the granulated sugar, and eggs.

Add sour cream and vanilla extract to the mixture and stir to combine.

Sift together flour, baking powder, and baking soda and fold into the wet ingredients.

Pour half of the cake batter into the greased baking dish and top with half of the package of chocolate chips.

Add the remaining half of the cake batter to the pan and top with the second half of the bag of chocolate chips.

Sprinkle the top of the cake with the remaining ¼ cup granulated sugar.

Bake the cake at 350°F for 30 minutes; insert a toothpick in the center of the cake to test doneness. If the toothpick comes out clean, remove the cake from the oven.

Let the cake cool completely before cutting into square pieces.

Lemon-Rosemary Gin Spritz

SERVES 1

A New Year's Day party should have a well-stocked bar. You need bottles of chilled champagne for those who are just starting the celebrations and some homemade Bloody Mary mix with all the fixings for friends who are nursing hangovers from the night before. This drink is a refreshing addition to the menu and a tasty alternative to the classic drinks on the New Year's bar cart. The cool piney flavor from gin and rosemary sprigs mixed with bright lemon citrus and sweet honey combine for a refreshing drink. Topping it with soda water makes it a bit lighter for daytime drinking, and not a bad option if you're looking to start those New Year's resolutions on day one. I also like to have a mocktail option on the bar cart for friends who aren't drinking (remember my pregnant New Year's Eve story?), and these ingredients blend well for a delicious sparkling drink if you make it without the gin.

While you're setting up the bar cart with all your cocktail ingredients and glassware, add a few party supplies to keep the party going from the night before. I place New Year's beads and horns and some New Year's glasses and crowns in big silver bowls or clear glass vases for a festive little addition to the celebration.

INGREDIENTS

2 ounces gin

½ ounce fresh lemon juice, plus lemon for garnish

½ ounce honey

Fresh rosemary sprigs

Soda water

INSTRUCTIONS

Add gin, fresh lemon juice, honey, and a rosemary sprig to a cocktail shaker over ice.

Shake the ingredients together vigorously and strain into a glass filled with ice.

Top the remainder of the glass with soda water and garnish with additional rosemary sprigs and lemons.

Tip

Scale this drink in a large batch for entertaining by multiplying the ingredients by the number of servings you'd like to have. Mix the gin, lemon juice, honey, and rosemary together and chill in a pitcher in the refrigerator before guests arrive. Serve with a bottle of soda water and garnishes on the side.

FAMILY GAME NIGHT MENU

Honey Butter Popcorn
Savory with Rosemary
Sweet with Cinnamon Sugar

Baked Cheese Straws
With Cheddar and Parmesan Cheese

Roasted Tomato Soup

Grilled Cheese Bar
With Crispy Baked Bacon

S'mores Rice Krispy Treats

Pomegranate Spice Cocktail

WHEN THE HOLIDAY DECORATIONS COME DOWN, AND THE NEW YEAR'S RESOLUTIONS HAVE BEEN ATTEMPTED AND ABANDONED, THERE'S STILL A LONG STRETCH OF WINTER AHEAD. Sometimes New England even likes to give us winter weather right through the end of April. Sometimes, it seems that on blustery and snowy weekends in February and March, there's not a single reason to go outside, so we just have to make some up.

A few of my favorite excuses to entertain in the winter: my birthday (why isn't that a national holiday yet?), "Galentine's" day gatherings, and awards show–viewing parties. Weekends away at mountain ski lodges are another wonderful reason to entertain. I don't ski but I love the idea of being snuggled up in a rustic cabin or mountain lodge, drinking hot cocoa and mulled wine. I think one of the best excuses for winter entertaining is getting snowed in with your family and hosting a cozy game night. I like to think of it as festive hibernation, and relish in having my crew at home for eating and drinking and fun by the fireplace.

Bring out the vintage board games, toss pillows on the floor, and turn off the Wi-Fi (just kidding, it'll be so cute you'll *definitely* want to Instagram it). I'm super competitive and love to play board games. As a kid our most-played board games were Clue and Trouble. Scrabble is my all-time favorite (writing nerd!), and a long afternoon playing Monopoly for hours on end with a cocktail in hand is an ideal way to spend a snow day. I love the games that get everyone up out of their seats and then falling over on the floor laughing.

One of the best things about hosting a game night is that you have built in decor for your party. Use old game boards under your food display as trays and trivets, take a pack of playing cards and use them for place cards with your guests' names written on the back, and use Scrabble tiles to spell out food labels and place in front of bowls and platters on the table. You could get very creative using game pieces as part of a tablescape; there are so many ways to make it look festive, fun, and a bit nostalgic too.

The nice thing about this type of casual winter entertaining, without a real holiday or event in mind, is that the expectations are low and the ambience is laid-back. It's about gathering around that warm fire, it's about warm wool sweaters and fluffy boot socks pulled up over leggings, it's about making your friends and family feel cozy and comfortable. What it means for a menu is simple comfort foods that give you that same warm feeling you get from snuggling up with a blanket to watch an old movie. Comfort food doesn't have to be heavy or rich, it just has to make your guests feel at home.

I'm all about creating comfort foods with a twist and presenting them in a way that looks good too. It could be as simple as making peanut butter and jelly sandwiches, but with really good homemade preserves and fluffy brioche bread, and serving them on a beautiful platter. The inspiration for this cozy winter menu is all about elevated comfort-food classics. Dress up big bowls of freshly popped popcorn with rustic herb and sweet seasoned butter drizzled on top. Make a childhood favorite like grilled cheese, but fill those sandwiches with indulgent crispy bacon and a sweet fig spread. Cut them up into little bite-size strips to dip into a warm, homemade roasted tomato soup. Serve fluffy, crunchy cheese straws dotted with flecks of savory seasonings. Take the food you grew up with and make it with love and care and delicious, quality ingredients.

Honey Butter Popcorn

Savory with Rosemary
Sweet with Cinnamon Sugar

SERVES 8

One of my favorite winter entertaining occasions is hosting my girlfriends (and occasionally a few guys too!) at our home for awards show viewing parties. It's a great excuse to avoid the Sunday-night-scaries, pop a bottle or two of champagne, and feast on snacks while judging celebrity ball gowns as we sit in our yoga pants. This recipe for freshly popped popcorn drizzled in warm flavored butters came from one of those nights. Popcorn is delicious, but we all know its true purpose: a vehicle for delivering warm melted butter. A flavored butter mixed with sweet honey and seasoning takes it to the next level.

Dividing the popcorn into two serving bowls gives you the chance to make a sweet honey butter flavored with cinnamon and sugar, and a more savory honey butter infused with fresh rosemary. It also means you have a better chance of grabbing a bite from a nearby bowl on the couch, and a bit more surface area for the butter drizzled on top. Have I mentioned I love butter? Make these for an afternoon of football viewing, snuggling on the couch with magazines, old movie marathons, or chilly weekend afternoons and you'll be everyone's favorite hostess.

INGREDIENTS

Plain popcorn
4 tablespoons (½ stick) butter, divided
4 tablespoons honey, divided
1 tablespoon chopped fresh rosemary
1 teaspoon cinnamon
1 teaspoon granulated sugar
Sea salt

INSTRUCTIONS

Prepare plain popcorn on stovetop as directed.

In a small saucepan, combine 2 tablespoons of the butter with 2 tablespoons of the honey and heat over medium heat until melted. Add chopped fresh rosemary to the butter and simmer for about 3 minutes.

In a second saucepan, combine remaining 2 tablespoons butter with 2 tablespoons honey and heat over medium heat until melted. Add cinnamon and sugar to the butter and simmer for about 3 minutes.

Place popcorn in two bowls, drizzle one with the rosemary honey butter and the other with the cinnamon sugar honey butter. Sprinkle both with sea salt to taste and serve immediately.

Tip

If you're hosting a large group, set out small popcorn boxes like you'd find at a movie theater with big bowls of popcorn drizzled with honey butter. You can find the popcorn boxes at most party stores. Add some fun mix-ins like nuts and candy so that guests can make their own popcorn mix to snack on for the night!

Baked Cheese Straws
With Cheddar and Parmesan Cheese
SERVES 12

Crispy baked cheese straws are one of the simplest appetizers to whip up for quick and casual entertaining. They're rustic-looking pastry dough twirled into puffy ribbons with sharp flavorful cheese, herbs, and spices folded in. Just a few ingredients are all you need to assemble these pretty straws.

INGREDIENTS

2 sheets frozen puff pastry, thawed

Flour, for dusting

1 large egg

½ cup grated cheddar cheese

½ cup grated Parmesan cheese

1 tablespoon chopped fresh parsley

1 tablespoon paprika

½ teaspoon salt

1 teaspoon cracked black pepper

INSTRUCTIONS

Preheat oven to 425°F. Line two baking sheets with parchment paper.

Roll out the thawed puff pastry sheets on a lightly floured work surface.

Beat one egg with a teaspoon of water, and use a brush to lightly coat the puff pastry sheets with the egg wash.

Combine cheddar cheese and Parmesan cheese, and sprinkle in a thin layer across the two puff pastry sheets.

Scatter finely chopped parsley across the pastry sheets; combine the paprika, salt, and pepper and sprinkle evenly over the pastry sheets.

Use your hands to lightly press the cheese, herbs, and seasoning down so that the ingredients stick to the dough.

Use a sharp knife or a pizza wheel to cut the dough into 1-inch-wide, long strips. Twist each strip and lay on baking sheets. Chill the strips in the refrigerator for 15 minutes to firm up the dough.

Bake at 425°F for 12–15 minutes, until lightly browned and puffed up. Remove from oven and cool on wire racks before serving.

Roasted Tomato Soup

SERVES 6

This version of the classic soup and sandwich combination uses roasted tomatoes and garlic, which brings out tons of sweetness in the ingredients. Blending in onions, shallots, red pepper, and Parmesan adds to the depth of flavor.

INGREDIENTS

1 pound tomatoes

¼ cup olive oil

Salt and black pepper

3–4 sprigs rosemary

1 head garlic

4 tablespoons (½ stick) butter, divided

1 large yellow onion

2 large shallots

1 (28-ounce) can whole peeled tomatoes

1 cup chicken broth

2 tablespoons tomato paste

2 teaspoons granulated sugar

1 teaspoon red pepper flakes

½ cup half-and-half

¼ cup Parmesan cheese, plus more for garnish

INSTRUCTIONS

Preheat oven to 450°F.

Cut tomatoes into quarters and scrape out seeds. Place them on a baking sheet, drizzle with olive oil and season with salt and pepper. Place rosemary sprigs to the top of the tomatoes.

Peel away any loose layers on the outside of the garlic head. Using a sharp knife, slice about ¼ inch off the top of the garlic head, leaving the tops of the cloves exposed. Place the head of garlic on a piece of aluminum foil and drizzle with olive oil and a bit of salt; wrap the edges of the foil up around the head of garlic to create a sealed packet. Add to the baking sheet with the tomatoes.

Roast at 450°F for 50–60 minutes; remove from oven when the tomatoes have burst and begin to char and garlic cloves have caramelized and softened. Remove and discard the rosemary sprigs after cooking.

Use a small fork to pull the roasted garlic cloves out of the head of garlic; add to the roasted tomatoes and set aside.

In a large dutch oven, melt 2 tablespoons of the butter over medium-high heat. Add minced onions and thinly sliced shallots to the pot and cook until softened, about 5–7 minutes.

Add roasted tomatoes, roasted garlic cloves, the can of tomatoes, chicken broth, and tomato paste to the pot; season with sugar and red pepper flakes. Cook for 15 minutes, until tomatoes start to break down.

Stir in the remaining 2 tablespoons butter, half-and-half, and Parmesan cheese and cook until heated through.

Use an immersion blender in the pot to puree the soup (you can also transfer the soup ingredients to a stand blender to puree). Blend until smooth.

Serve hot and garnish with fresh herbs; pair with crispy baked cheese straws and grilled cheese sandwiches.

Grilled Cheese Bar
With Crispy Baked Bacon
SERVES 4

Getting your guests involved in food assembly is totally acceptable if you call something a "bar"—like an "assemble your own Bloody Mary bar" or "make your own taco bar." You've done the hard work of gathering and presenting the ingredients, toppings, and garnishes, and it's time for them to roll up their sleeves and produce their own culinary creation out of the tools you've given them. Maybe I'm just being lazy making my guests do the hard work of putting together their own drink or taco or sandwich, but I like to think of it as interactive. Everyone gets involved and gets the exact meal they want!

For a wintry do-it-yourself lunch bar, I envisioned endless stacks of buttery, toasted, gooey grilled cheeses coming off a hot griddle. Set it up with all sorts of delicious breads and cheeses so that guests can make their ideal grilled cheese sandwich—the possibilities are endless and mouthwateringly satisfying.

The recipe I'm sharing here is for a grilled cheese with a combination of cheddar and American cheeses, a sweet fig spread, and crispy bacon on a fluffy brioche. The key to an amazing grilled cheese is marrying the best ingredients. I used a combination of cheeses for flavor and their melting capabilities. Cheddar is sharp and hearty, while the American cheese is smooth and melts perfectly

Favorite Loaded Grilled Cheese Combos

Provolone cheese, sautéed spinach, and caramelized onions

Pepper Jack cheese, avocado, and red pepper flakes

Brie, honey, and prosciutto

American cheese, crispy maple bacon, and tomato slices

Mozzarella, roasted tomatoes, and fresh basil

Apple slices, gruyère, and cheddar cheese

Swiss cheese and sautéed mushrooms

Triple cheese: cheddar, American, and Swiss cheeses

in a grilled cheese. The fig spread is something that you can usually find at the grocery store near the jams and jellies, or tucked in near the cheese section. Figs have a sweet flavor and caramelize a bit in the grilled cheese under heat. The bread, a fluffy brioche, soaks in the butter and toasts up well on the griddle.

The bacon needs to be thick and crispy for a good grilled cheese. I have a secret trick for ensuring that every bite of the grilled cheese gets a bit of bacon in it too! I weave the bacon like a lattice piecrust and bake it in the oven to cook into a large bacon sheet. Once it comes out of the oven, it cools on a paper towel to soak up some of the fat and set into a solid piece of woven bacon lattice. Then I cut the bacon lattice into square pieces that will match the size of the bread I'm making our grilled cheeses on. You'll get a crisp piece of bacon in every single bite of the grilled cheese.

Another trick to making a picture-perfect grilled cheese is to use just a tiny bit of mayonnaise spread on the outside of the bread. It sounds weird, but it really works. A tiny layer of mayonnaise on the bread before you drop it on the hot, buttery griddle or skillet results in perfect golden browning and a rich, tangy note to the final sandwich. If you're not convinced, make it the classic way with butter, white bread, and American cheese. At my grilled cheese bar, it's totally up to you to make it how you like it!

INGREDIENTS

1 pound thick-cut bacon

4 tablespoons (½ stick) butter, divided

2 tablespoons mayonnaise

8 slices brioche bread

4 tablespoons fig spread

8 slices sharp cheddar cheese

8 slices American cheese

INSTRUCTIONS

Preheat oven to 375°F.

On a large rimmed baking sheet lined with parchment paper, arrange five or six slices of bacon in horizontal lines. Take the remaining five or six pieces of bacon and place them vertically over the horizontal strips. Weave the bacon together in a lattice pattern, like you're assembling a lattice piecrust.

Bake at 375°F for 30 minutes, until crispy, then remove from oven and transfer to a paper towel–lined cutting board to rest.

After resting for 10 minutes, remove the paper towel and cut the bacon lattice into four square-shaped pieces.

Heat a skillet or griddle over medium heat; melt 2 tablespoons of the butter in the pan.

Spread a thin layer of mayonnaise on the outside of all 8 slices of bread. Add a thin layer of fig spread to the inside of all 8 slices of bread.

Stack two slices of cheddar cheese, two slices of American cheese, and the square bacon lattices on four of the pieces of brioche, top with the other four bread slices to make the sandwiches.

Place the sandwiches, mayonnaise side down, into the hot pan. When the underside is golden brown, about 4 minutes, add remaining 2 tablespoons butter to the skillet or griddle and turn sandwiches to finish cooking.

Press down on the sandwich lightly with the back of a spatula to help melt the cheese, and watch for the second side to turn golden brown.

Once the grilled cheeses are evenly toasted and the cheese is fully melted, remove from the pan.

Eat immediately while hot. Slice into halves or small dipping strips that can be served with roasted tomato soup.

Tip

If you're hosting a DIY bar of any type, whether it's grilled cheeses, signature cocktails, or building your own tacos, it can be helpful to add a menu board with suggested ideas to push guests in the right direction or spark ideas they may not have thought of! Write it up on a chalkboard, or print out options and place them in a small frame on the buffet table.

S'mores Rice Krispy Treats

SERVES 8–12

I consider Rice Krispy treats my signature dish. I've made countless shapes and flavor combinations, but this recipe is perhaps my greatest Rice Krispy achievement. With marshmallow as the flavor base of these crunchy sweet bites, adding chocolate and graham crackers to the mix was a no-brainer.

Always remember the 5:7:5 formula—you should always have five tablespoons of butter, seven cups of marshmallows, and five cups of Rice Krispies cereal. Swap ingredients in and out of this ratio to experiment with the resulting flavors. In this recipe, to account for the addition of graham crackers, the amount of Rice Krispies cereal was reduced. This magic ratio is the key to Rice Krispy treat success!

Use mini marshmallows for the best ooey-gooey results. They melt faster and more evenly into the butter and create a smoother texture overall. Stir frequently to keep the marshmallow-butter mixture from burning, and remove it from the heat when you start to fold in the cereal to prevent the Rice Krispies from cooking (and softening). Let it fully rest and firm up before cutting into squares and you'll get crisp, clean bites of Rice Krispy treats that will have your friends and family begging you to make more!

INGREDIENTS

5 tablespoons butter

7 cups mini marshmallows

Dash of sea salt

4 cups Rice Krispies cereal

1 cup crushed graham crackers, divided

⅓ cup mini chocolate chips

INSTRUCTIONS

Line a 9- x 9-inch baking dish with parchment paper.

Melt butter over medium heat; stir in the mini marshmallows and sea salt as it melts.

Stir the mixture constantly as it heats until all the marshmallows are fully melted and combined with the butter.

Remove the butter-marshmallow mixture from the heat and quickly fold in the Rice Krispies cereal and ¾ cup of the crushed graham crackers.

Press the mixture into a rimmed baking dish.

Sprinkle the remaining graham cracker crumbs and chocolate chips onto the top of the Rice Krispy treats, and use a second piece of parchment paper to press them down into the warm marshmallows so that they stick.

Let the Rice Krispy treats rest, loosely covered with parchment paper, for at least an hour at room temperature before cutting into squares.

Transfer to a serving plate and cover tightly with plastic wrap until ready to serve.

Pomegranate Spice Cocktail

SERVES 6

Pomegranates are one of the most visually inspiring ingredients I've ever come across—the deep red tone, the clusters of juicy gem-like seeds inside, even the stem at the top looks like a little mini crown atop this regal fruit. This pomegranate-infused simple syrup—full of wintry spice from the cloves and sweet flavors from the honey and sugar—was inspired by the beautiful fruit it's made with. The bold taste and color are all you need to make simple sparkling cocktails with a bit of prosecco. The leftover pomegranate seeds make a beautiful garnish, and I like to slice open a few pomegranates with the seeds intact to decorate the bar area where I'm serving drinks—they look so good you'll want to eat (or sip!) them up.

INGREDIENTS

¼ cup pomegranate seeds, plus more for garnish

½ fresh lemon, sliced

¼ cup granulated sugar

½ cup water

1 tablespoon honey

1 teaspoon whole cloves

Prosecco

INSTRUCTIONS

In a small saucepan, combine pomegranate seeds, sliced lemon, sugar, water, honey, and cloves.

Heat mixture for 20 minutes over medium heat until all the sugar has dissolved.

Remove from heat and strain the liquid into a glass container; discard seeds, lemon, and spices.

Chill the syrup for about 20 minutes before serving.

To serve, pour 1 tablespoon syrup into a cocktail glass and top with chilled prosecco; garnish with fresh pomegranate seeds.

ACKNOWLEDGMENTS

To my loving, supportive, crazy family, I love you so much.

Mom, this book quite literally wouldn't exist if it weren't for you. Thank you for the endless amounts of free babysitting, folded laundry, and dishwashing that you took on so that I could work on this project. You helped make my dreams come true, which you selflessly told me is just what moms do. You are the best. Dad, thank you for teaching me the value of hard work and the importance of following your passion; you are the embodiment of the phrase "work hard, play hard," and I'm so happy you taught me how to do the same.

Pete and Mara, thank you for your love and your humor, and for always being available to play the *"If you could have one food in the world right now . . ."* game. Mara, a special thank you for being my constant and earliest cheerleader; you encouraged me to hit publish for the very first time, and I'm so grateful to have a sister like you. Alex, thank you for sharing your good olive oil and prosciutto.

To my Bowler crew—Ed, Sue, Katie, Mike, and Bri—I'm so lucky to have you in my corner. Your constant love and support (and eagerness to help with taste testing) mean the world to me. To my amazing grandmothers: Ida and Anne. You have both taught me, each in your very own and different ways, about being a strong woman and a fabulous hostess. I love you both. To my girls: Colleen, Krista, Navya, and Taz, thank you for your endless encouragement and love; you are truly remarkable friends, you are my family.

Thank you to the team at Globe Pequot who took a chance on me and made this idea a reality. A special thanks to Katie O'Dell; I'm so grateful for your guidance in developing this book.

Finally, to my amazing little family, my home team, I love you. Janie-Bean, my little foodie baby, your big appetite and your big heart are my everything; all of this hard work is for you. To my wonderful husband, you are an endless source of encouragement, support, and inspiration. Most people would have called me crazy when I said I was going to write and photograph a cookbook in four months while running a business and taking care of an infant. But not you; you told me to say yes, take the leap, and we'd figure it all out together. I've been able to take big leaps because I know that when I do, you're holding my hand and jumping with me. You are my best friend, and I love you more than anything.

INDEX

ABOUT THE AUTHOR

Kate Bowler is the author of the popular lifestyle blog Domestikatedlife .com, where she writes about festive entertaining tips, adventures in home cooking, DIY projects, and life as a new mom. Her work has been featured in *Martha Stewart Living*, *Better Homes and Gardens*, *Family Circle*, and many other publications. She lives in a charming coastal town outside of Boston with her husband and their daughter. You can find her online at @domestikateblog.

Madeline Rose Photography